Phileas Phil, Around The World In 65 Days

By Philip Hill

First Published in 2022 by Blossom Spring Publishing
Phileas Phil, Around The World In 65 Days
© 2022 Philip Hill
ISBN 978-1-7398866-5-3
E: admin@blossomspringpublishing.com
W: www.blossomspringpublishing.com

Day 1 London to Berlin

In which having decided to go; there was no point turning back

"Phileas Fogg, having shut the door of his house at half-past eleven, and having put his right foot before his left five hundred and seventy-five times, and his left foot before his right five hundred and seventy-six times, reached the Reform Club." - Jules Verne

Scared is perhaps too strong a word, but nervous, yes, I was nervous. I was taking the *Eurostar* from London to Brussels. I hoped to finish my day in Berlin. Day one of a dive into the dark. I was calm, quiet, and honestly, a tad nervous. I thought I may feel elated, excited at the prospect of what lay ahead, but I wasn't. I was flat. I think sitting at St. Pancras waiting to board my train, the enormity of what I was embarking on started to crowd in on me.

An hour earlier my daughter had dropped me off at the station, after a brief stop at the Reform Club, the starting point for Phileas Fogg's journey around the world. Quite why I felt it necessary to go there I'm not sure, but I did, and I did! And I vowed to return in less than 80 days, just like good old Phileas.

It's easy to now consider that there was a lot that could go wrong with this journey. Had Phileas such worries as he calmly returned to his home in Saville Row, gathered a few possessions and set off for the station? No, he appeared to rise above such trepidation. This was a man who was never *upset* or *disturbed*. A man who would face any adversity with *"stillness in the midst of agitation"*.

My journey involved many different stages, and a lot of them made with very loose planning. Hindsight, as they say, is a wonderful thing. I had worked on the over-riding belief that if it all went pear-shaped, I could just quit, call it a day, and find the nearest airport to fly home. It wasn't my plan, but there was always as a possibility. At that time, sitting with my two pieces of luggage and ready to embark, I never realised it would only take three days for the pear to show its shape.

I'm a bit of a loner. Not a recluse or anti-social, it's just that I am comfortable with my own company. Being alone would not be an issue, but loneliness may be. I'm not sure why, but sitting on that platform, waiting to board that train was the loneliest I was to feel throughout the whole trip. Letting go of comfort and security for what? A crazy harebrained plan to emulate a fictional character from a 140-year-old book. Really, what was going on in my head?

As my daughter dropped me at the station, she asked when she would see me again. I didn't know how to answer her, I just smiled, gave her a hug, and said farewell. As I waved goodbye to her on that cold, damp London morning, for the briefest of moments I considered hailing a black cab and going home. In only 30 minutes I could be there, and I'd be drinking a coffee with some toast and watching the early morning news on TV before going back to bed. After all, I didn't need to do this. I had nothing to prove to myself or anyone else. This was whimsical. What was I doing? Honestly, I can say, I didn't know.

But I didn't go home, I marched off into the station, and made my way to the platform, and the start of a trip I would never forget and never want to. This was adventure, and I was a modern-day Phileas Fogg.

The journey loosely fell into five segments. London to Moscow, then the Trans-Siberian Railway to Beijing, more trains to Hong Kong. Honkers to Los Angeles, across America until finally the Atlantic back to Europe. I had chosen this route as it was a lifetime ambition to travel the Trans-Siberian - images from *Dr Zhivago*, Omar Sharif playing a Russian, braving the cold. He must have missed the heat of Egypt making that movie. And cold it would certainly prove to be. And the *Orient Express* it would prove not to be.

The ocean crossings had interested me. Tricky but doable. And crossing the U.S. would be fun, as I intended to include some cities not previously visited - San Diego and Chicago. But first I had to reach Berlin, another city on my hit-list. How is it I had travelled so extensively globally, and within Germany, and yet missed Berlin? Sometimes we don't know our own backyard. I wanted to see the *Wall*, or what was left of it.

"It was pitch dark, and it was drizzling with rain. Phileas Fogg, sitting in his corner, didn't say a word."

It was 6:50 a.m. and I was on my way. My train crawled away from the station before picking up pace. No turning back, I thought. Two days later I did turn back, but then turned again. Heading east, always east, and like Phileas, gaining a day halfway across the world in the middle of the Pacific Ocean.

If everything went according to plan, I should reach the former colony of Hong Kong in 15 days. Trains, trains, and more trains. I never took trains, or at least hadn't for years. Suddenly I was becoming an *anorak*. When this journey was over, I would always embrace the chance to travel by train. *Let the train take the strain*, was a slogan from a 1980's TV advertisement, and never had it been truer. I was letting the train take the strain all the way to the *MV Hanjin Athens* and the Pacific Ocean, which I hoped was waiting to take me to the New World.

A tunnel took me out of England and onto the

3

continent. An island nation pretending to be part of the bigger picture, part of a Europe some hoped to one day leave. And leave we did, but only politically, once a European always a European! And those Europeans know a thing or two about trains. In Brussels, as I swapped the *Eurostar* for the *Ice 15*, even the name was cool, excuse the pun! It was a Belgian or perhaps German version of the Japanese bullet, very sleek, the anoraks may even say sexy. There were no lower luggage racks, so suitcases were blocking the aisles. They had clearly gone for style over substance. After an hour German efficiency was brought into question, *Ice 15* had a hiccup and broke down. Thank God it wasn't a Swiss train, there would have been a national inquiry!

I finally reached Cologne but missed my connection to Berlin. Day one was already looking a bit sketchy, but nothing compared to day three which was an absolute humdinger.

A few hours later, arriving in a cold and snowy Berlin, I felt a sense of satisfaction at my first day going to schedule. Christmas was approaching so the Weihnachtsmärkte would be loving all this white. After checking into my very average hotel, I sought one out. It didn't take long, they are on almost every street corner that time of year, those Christmas markets.

I'm not sure why the good folks of Germany love Christmas markets. They all sell the same old same old. And along with BMWs and Bosch appliances they have now exported them to the rest of Europe. In the U.K. we can now find clusters of wooden huts, with their fake snow roofs, selling that same old, and steaming wine. And we diligently join in. Tradition, that's why they do it, and now it's become a tradition for us and so many others. Imported Christmas tradition, along with

Christstollen and Italian Panettone. No Christmas would now be complete without those little gems.

After joining the throng for some gluhwein and wurst I returned to my hotel and hit the sack. But before dropping off, I sat and wrote my journal. I was not sure why. I'm not a diary writer, and I had never kept such a record of any other journey I had made. But like so much about this one, I was venturing into the unknown. I decided to keep a written record of as much as possible on my journey around the world. That journal forms the basis for this book. So, I diligently sat and wrote, as I did every day until it was all over. It had been a long and exhausting first day, but it had gone according to plan, and I was well and truly on my way.

Day 2 Berlin

In which a new city is discovered, and an old acquaintance renewed

"Mr. Gorbachev, open this gate! Mr. Gorbachev, tear down this wall!" - Ronald Reagan

Berlin was a new city to me. Images of Liza Minelli with her provocative stockings, suspenders and bowler hat in *Cabaret*, and escapees being shot clambering to freedom from east to west filled my mind. But this was the new Berlin, the restored capital of the *Fatherland*. No longer a dividing wall between the superpowers, no longer swastikas flying from the Reichstag; no, those were the *good old days*. Today the city was one of youth and art and a newfound belief in the unity of people from all nations. That little Austrian postman would turn in his grave, hearing English so widely spoken in the city of his purest race.

And, on the subject of swastikas, one wonders how such an ancient symbol for *good fortune*, could be abused to become a symbol of evil. Potent things, symbols. Flags, walls, memorials, Berlin had it all and much more. The setting for Len Deighton and John Le Carré in so many novels, the aptly named *Funeral in Berlin*. My anticipation at movie recall was high. David Bowie *"Had to catch a train from Potsdamer Platz"*, and that was my goal tomorrow morning - catching a train from Potsdamer Platz, heading east to an eventual meeting with the Siberian tundra. Mr Bowie was singing in my ears all day.

I had been looking forward to this day for many years. Berlin, just the name got the tourist juices flowing. It had somehow passed me by, this city, but not now, not today. I was here and intended to see all that I could. An old friend, Helga, had offered to show me around her city, and she had a lot to show, and not much time to show it. The whistle stop tour started just after 8 a.m. I'd met Helga a year earlier in Greece, where she was on a three-month student programme to learn organic farming. She hadn't changed much. Blue eyed, and blonde haired, Helga was every outsider's vision of what a German *fraulein* should look like. Being a 30-year-old-plus student seemed to be the fashion in this city. Why work when you can study? I wasn't certain how much organic farming she would get up to in the middle Berlin!

She marched me around at pace, and if there was a site to be seen, I saw it. The Wall, or what is left of it, still holds a deep-rooted power to disturb. The bit I saw had Brezhnev kissing Honecker, they call it *The Kiss of Death*. They looked happy enough to me. Clearly, they hadn't bargained on Gorbachev upsetting the apple cart. The Wall should be a great reminder of the futility of such structures. But a few years later I was to see a newer, still *active*, wall in Bethlehem, Israel a few hundred metres from the birthplace of Christ. He sure wouldn't have been happy to see that monstrosity. That wall is also full of graffiti, and it doesn't make pleasant reading - no kissing going on there.

And on that subject, Berlin's *Memorial to the Murdered Jews of Europe* should make us all realise that there are two sides to every story. Close to *Checkpoint Charlie* we did the splits with a foot each in the east and west. Lines of division. I have visited a few *lines* over the years, Nicosia and Belfast coming to mind. They are still active, those two lines. Progress can be quite slow when you think about it.

My afternoon afforded me a treat. I was transported back to the Cold War era. We visited the Stasi Museum.

A large yellow/grey building which could pass as a regular office block. Lots of corridors and rooms filled with all manner of gadgets aimed at tripping up Harry Palmer and James Bond. Didn't Honecker and his boys understand that it would take more than a few hidden cameras to catch out the MI6 elite? And those gadgets were hidden everywhere. A camera in the button of a trench coat, a listening device in a wristwatch. Spying must be so boring these days; a mobile phone holds more capability than the whole of that building. I mean, you can buy a fibre optic camera on Amazon for ten euros. What was even cooler than the gadgets were the furniture. Some of those chairs could fetch thousands in the hipster stores of the East End of London.

My day came to an end as I said my farewells to Helga. She had been a wonderful guide, showing me the essentials, and a couple of non-essentials. I felt quite at home in Berlin. I consider myself *arty*, and the vibe there was great. But time was pressing on me, and my schedule couldn't afford me another day in this lively city. It had got under my skin, and I knew I was only skimming the surface. There is a vibe that resonates with me, and I want it to soak into me, this passing glimpse was not enough. I determined to return one day and spend more time here. Little did I know it would be much sooner than I expected. Fate and my stupidity would soon be playing a sleight of hand to catch me out.

Helga sent me on my way after a couple of beers and a *currywurst*, which also had a trick all of its own to deliver.

Phileas Fogg had chosen ships for the majority of his attempt to win his bet of £20,000. Trains to Brindisi in Italy and then ships to India. I had opted for trains to reach Hong Kong. Today that sum would amount to about £2,500,000, so that was some gamble. He spent the same amount during his journey, buying elephants and ships along the way to ensure he won the bet and arrived back in London in 80 days. Satisfying my *wanderlust* and completing my journey was to cost about £10,000 in total. I always look back and think what incredible value for money. I saw the world for far less than you would spend on a motor vehicle. You can book a world cruise for about the same money, but it will take longer than 80 days.

The following morning, I was due to catch an early morning train, very early - 4 a.m. - for an overnight journey to Moscow via Poland and Belarus. I was looking forward to a quiet couple of days peacefully trundling through the eastern European greyness to my destiny with the Trans-Siberian railway, and the fulfilment of a life-long ambition. Those quiet days were anything but and, if what was to follow was peaceful, then to misquote JFK (it really does not mean what people interpret it as), *Ich bin ein Berliner*. Because actually, I really was a doughnut!

Day 3 Berlin to Belarus

Where Phileas Phil proves himself equal to the situation

"The wisest thing to do if you're living in hell is to make yourself comfortable." - Charles Bukowski

I could hear the unmistakeable sound of heavy boots running in my direction. I knew they were coming for me, and all I could do was sit and wait those few seconds before they burst into my compartment. I was on a train and had reached the Poland-Belarus border. They didn't disappoint me, those boots. In the fateful seconds before their arrival, I was thankful for the dodgy *currywurst* I had eaten the evening before in a Berlin Christmas market, as it had reaped its revenge on me this morning. Thankful, because it meant my now quivering bowels were empty and I would not embarrass myself in the face of an unpleasant, as Donald Rumsfeld would say, *"Unknown unknown."*

The Belarusian border guard that reached me first, those few seconds later, I had seen before. But this time, unlike the last and, as if by magic, he produced a *blue* ink pad and rubber stamp from his tunic pocket. Casually, and I would swear he was either smirking, or was scared that he had made a cock-up, he said, 'Passport.' I knew this was not going to end well. By now three of his soldier buddies had crowded in on the scene. Me and four of them, the odds were stacking up against me.

Rewind five minutes and my friendly border guard had produced a *red* ink pad and stamp, and happily accepted that my Trans-Siberian train ticket for the following day was sufficient for me to transit his wonderful country to reach Moscow. Clearly there had been a rethink. My lovely red transit stamp had now

10

been covered with a blue stamp; ANULVANA. Cancelled. This leg of my journey around the world was proving to be tricky, and, in my meticulous planning, I had considered this the easy part.

I must have gone into meltdown because I cannot remember what immediately followed but, as if *beamed up* by Scotty on Star Trek, my next conscious recollection of events is that I was in a minibus with eight Belarusian soldiers. Armed to the teeth. Scowling at me. I cleared the window next to me with my coat sleeve to find it was dark, snowing and very cold. I noticed a digital clock which switched display with the temperature. It read -7c outside, it felt the same inside. I was surprisingly calm, perhaps taking inspiration from Michael Caine, straight out of a Len Deighton spy novel. It was very clear to me that the train I had been on, the one taking me to Moscow, was now rattling past me as it moved off. Getting to Moscow was not going to be as easy as I originally thought. That train was going to reach its destination without me, and I was heading - well actually I had no idea where I was heading.

There were lessons to be learned from this predicament, but whilst freezing to death in this 1960s cold war movie scene in which I found myself, I was not sure what they were. Something to do with more thorough research before you try to emulate a fictional adventurer. He managed the journey I was embarking on in 80 days. I planned to do it in less than 70, but was this situation going to force me to abandon my attempt? For goodness' sake, it was only day three! My only rational, or perhaps irrational, thought was getting myself out of this mess and flying home. Dear old Phileas would be laughing his head off, but then he didn't even need a passport when he set off, although he did take one and get it stamped to prove where he had been. I now had proof in my passport of what an idiot I was! Any would-be adventurers reading this please note, doing your homework pays dividends.

We didn't travel very far, so I figured I was just across the border, somewhere in Belarus. As I later discovered, it turned out to be about a very short, but possibly my longest, ten kilometres. The minibus journey was a blur, no one spoke. I was stared at occasionally. I guess it gave the boys something to do. They could go home and tell the wife about their exciting day with the dumb Englishman over that evening's *borsch*. No one made a move to shoot me or pull my fingernails out. My calmness worried me, I should have been having kittens, or at least protesting my outrage and innocence, 'Don't you know I'm British? Call the embassy immediately.' But I said nothing, I sat there, dumbstruck - like a lemon. Days later I reflected that I had called upon some unbeknown hidden calmness reserves from some previous difficult predicaments - Beirut airport came to mind, another *visa* situation. I guess the more you face in life the more prepared you are when you are thrown a curve ball. Right now, the curve ball felt like a bowling ball.

Perhaps I should clarify at this point, I am not a member of any government agency, a secret enforcement group nor anything wildly exotic or even mildly interesting. I'm just a regular man in my mid-fifties. Yes, I like travel, and yes, I like a *good old journey* rather than a beach resort and all-inclusive cocktails by the pool with sunburned tourists, but I am really not used to this kind of *cloak and dagger* stuff. I've had a few *misunderstandings* in the past, but I follow the rules and don't break any laws - well at least no more than the next man. So, this mess that I now found myself in was something *out of the ordinary*, and I was definitely not getting a buzz from it. In fact, when I have ever spoken about it, I feel like I'm recounting the details in the third person, 'and then he did this, and then he did that'. Like it is not really me, because me, well I never considered a life in the movie *Spy Game,* that's for people like Brad Pitt and Robert Redford.

Finally, I was deposited in a large, sparse hall. At first, I could not make out the purpose of the hall. Was it a government building? I was pretty confident that, at least, it was not a police station or prison. I was left alone. Me and my two bags in a very large hall. I consciously tried to recover my composure. 'Think,' I told myself. I realised I still had my telephone. No one had searched me or taken anything away from me. I still had my passport. Michael Caine would have made a run for it. Jason Bourne would have escaped from the minibus without seeing the hall - he probably wouldn't have let them put him in the minibus to begin with. I sat with my phone in my hand wondering what I should do. After considering my options I decided to make a call. I looked up and a soldier, I guess he was my guard, on the far side of the hall, was staring at me. I smiled. Stupid thing to do really. I held up the phone in one hand and an index finger on the other. He glared for a few seconds and then nodded. That nod told me a lot. It told me I was going to get out of this mess. Well at least that's what I told myself, and that made me feel a whole lot better. So, I decided, I'd *phone a friend.* I remember laughing at that thought - clearly my nervousness was beginning to manifest. My mate Magnus answered but my relief was short-lived when he said, 'I can't speak now I'm at a yacht club meeting in London.' 'Wait!' I shouted, in near panic, before he cut me off. The guard moved a fraction in the corner of my eye. I looked up and smiled again, and he settled back in his chair.

Magnus waited. I explained my current situation in as few words as possible, fearful he would hang up. I heard him laugh, and then utter disbelief followed by a series of expletives. Magnus is a practical sort, Danish, but living in England for 30 years - those years hadn't made him any less Danish, cool as a cucumber those Scandinavians. That's why I called him. He knew how to stay cool. 'Why isn't he here instead of me?' I thought. 'Tell me what to do?' he said. I did. I was thinking fast, which was probably not a good thing to do, given the circumstances. I told him I would call back in two hours, if I could.

Time stood still. I realised I was thirsty and hungry; I must have left my water bottle and snacks on the train. What I would have given for a cup of tea at that moment, or even better a shot of vodka. Suddenly there was a mechanical noise outside. I jumped. It's fair to say my nerves were frazzled. Externally I must have, or at least hoped that I appeared calm, but internally I was in a tailspin. What was on my agenda next, a cell for the night, or maybe a simple deportation? Every conceivable scenario went through my mind.

It was a train, the mechanical noise. The hall was a train station. The situation was getting more promising. Would another red ink pad be produced and send me on my way to Moscow? If only I had known what false hope I was creating, and what nightmare lay ahead of me. Day four was going to prove very challenging.

A couple of soldiers appeared and joined my guard, they exchanged a few words, looked over at me and then headed my way. It was indicated, through a lot of pointing and grunting, that I should gather my luggage. We were off somewhere. No one spoke any English to me, actually no one spoke at all. It was as though we all knew our roles in this drama, and as if, in a perfectly choreographed performance, we all went through the motions. Being lead actor, I should have known what was going on, alas I had not read the script and just improvised.

I was ushered onto a platform where there was what I can only describe as a wooden train. It was something straight out of the wild west and that made me a cowboy, albeit I was the only person without a gun. The last time I had seen anything like it was in Soller on Mallorca. That journey I had enjoyed; this one was not giving me the same vibes. A door was opened, and I was invited to climb aboard. The inside was even more wood and ridiculously I remember wondering why a train would be made of wood in these temperatures, whilst also marvelling at how warm the carriage was. The carriage could hold about fifty people, but I had it all to myself. Lucky me. Only half an hour later did I discover the train was almost full. I was possibly travelling Belarusian first class, although it appeared more like fourth, if such a train class exists.

There were no handshakes or salutes goodbye. In fact, nothing passed between me and the soldiers. The train started to move, and I watched them turn away as this little charade was over for the night. They were headed home for some hot *borsch* and a couple of vodkas. I was not the first and would not be the last acting out this play. No words had been necessary as this was a well-rehearsed scene. Only I was this night's stand in and had never played the role before. I think I did okay. I had not added too many theatricals, no screaming and shouting; my only form of communication had been a single index finger request. Belarusians were not such a bad lot, no thumb screws, they just didn't like foreigners showing up without a transit visa, even if no one in their right mind would have wanted to get off that train on a snowy freezing night in the middle of nowhere.

The *Wild West* express slowly chugged away into the night and I was breathing a huge sigh of relief which, as it turned out, was to be very short-lived.

About 15 minutes later the train stopped, doors were being opened. I looked out of the window. The whole train was disgorging onto a frozen platform. When you don't know what to do, be a lemming, follow the crowd. I got off with everyone else. This was a good thing as the train was going nowhere other than back the way it came, and I certainly had no desire to do that, although it could have been funny showing up back at the station where I boarded. 'Hello guys, I really missed this place, nice to see you again.'

They were a miserable looking lot, the passengers, but I was surely the most miserable of all. They knew where they were and what they were doing, I had no idea. I assumed the Polish border, but which one?

Warsaw, I had to reach Warsaw, at least from there I could work something out. It was eight in the evening - the clock was ticking. My train across Siberia departed at midnight the following day. I had to be on it. Travelling around the world has a schedule that needs to be maintained, and I was three days in and blowing it. I had been determined not to fly. Flying would be easy, 48 hours would do it. I realised I would have to fly to Moscow if I was to make that train. And I was definitely going to make it. Didn't Phileas fly in a balloon at some point, perhaps over Paris? Perhaps that was the film, not the book - I had forgotten to take it with me! I was hugely disappointed at the thought of flying, it wasn't what I had planned, but I figured if I could make it to Moscow around the same time as my original train was due to arrive, I could justify the *needs must* approach. I was not happy about it at all, but I was out of options. There and then I vowed to myself that for the rest of the journey I would not fly again. If the need arose, I would bail out and fly home. And the truth is I didn't fly again, and there were times I really did want to bail out, but I didn't do that either - but I'm getting ahead of myself. I was in *no-man's land*. I had to find out where I was, and how I was going to reach Moscow in time - in fact, just getting to Warsaw would be nice.

I was at the back of the queue at an outside immigration cabin. Terespol, Eastern Poland, that's where I was. I'd never heard of it, and if there was a god in heaven, I never would again - so hopefully my first and last visit. I was being snowed on. I was cold, thirsty, and hungry, and was utterly miserable. I was looking for adventure and if this wasn't it, what was? But right now, the all-inclusive with cocktails thrown in seemed like a wonderful idea.

I finally cleared immigration and tried to buy a ticket to Warsaw. It was zloty or zloty, they wouldn't take credit cards, euros or dollars. I asked around if anyone would like some dollars, I was offering the best exchange rate in history. Warren Buffet would have snatched my hand off. After five minutes a grumpy old man finally made me an offer I couldn't refuse; survival. I virtually gave him the dollars. Fortunately, the zloty were enough to get me to Warsaw and buy a bottle of water. Moving away from that border made me feel good, but I was full of apprehension for what lay ahead.

As if the day had not been surreal enough, two hours later I found myself watching the Bond film *Skyfall* on my phone, together with a beautiful blonde Polish girl, Maja. Would I ever forget this day? It was certainly proving to be one of highs and lows. We were on my second train since leaving Terespol, arriving at Warsaw around eleven thirty that night.

I had been considering my options, following another chat with Magnus in London, when I bumped, literally, into Maja on the platform where I changed trains. Maja was the only good thing to happen in Biala Podlaska; in fact, she was the only good thing to happen that day, week, and month. A couple of hours later, just as M was popping her clogs in the Scottish Highlands, I reached a decision about how I would get from Warsaw to Moscow. There were several factors influencing this decision, and none of them filled me with enthusiasm. It was some 30 minutes later as the train pulled into Warsaw, Maja threw a spanner in the works by suggesting I stay the night with her and fly to Moscow the next day from there. That had not been an option I considered when I made my earlier decision but, on the face of it, reconsideration would not have been unreasonable. My problem was that accepting such a proposal would almost certainly mean I would miss my connection in Moscow, because I would struggle to leave Warsaw, and that would throw the whole adventure out of the window. Was I really going to decline the beautiful Maja's offer? I mean, did I not deserve some light entertainment after such an evening? But decline I did. She gave me her number in case I changed my mind. It was 35 minutes later as I sat in a cramped, smoky, over-heated train compartment with seven drunken Poles heading into a snowy wilderness that I realised what a complete and utter fool I was.

Maja was one of those people you meet from time to time who are just *nice*. She had probably seen what effect the stress of my predicament was having on me, and she wanted to help. Perhaps no more than that. Travelling threw up many surprises to me over the years, but the over-riding one, and the one that always affected me so much, was that there were so many good people out there just waiting to be met and wanting to help. The media would have us believe there is a serial killer on every corner, the truth is there is a good Samaritan on every corner, we just have to open our eyes to see them. I would think about Maja in the following days, and probably long after she had forgotten me. Hopefully when she next watched a Bond movie, she might remember the idiot Englishman who tried to transit Belarus without a visa. James Bond I was certainly not!

It was just before midnight. I stood on the platform of Warsaw's main station waiting for the train that would take me on a seriously bizarre route, involving further three trains, back to Berlin, back to where I had started the day. I had faced tough, complex choices and plumped for the one that gave me the best possible guarantee. I knew there was a flight at midday the following day from Berlin to Moscow. I knew this because my travelling companion for the Trans-Siberian railway, Sofia, would be on that airplane, and she would not have appreciated arriving in Moscow only to discover I wasn't there. But as I stood on that platform watching the train pull in, I can honestly say I was the most nervous I had been all day. And as it turned out I had very good reason.

Travel Tip: if taking a train from Europe to Moscow and crossing Belarus, be sure to obtain a transit visa before entering the country!

Day 4 Warsaw to Moscow

When discovering who one can trust proves essential if what looks impossible is to be made possible

"Only through suffering can we find ourselves." - Fyodor Dostoevsky

By now my nerves were shredded. Five minutes ago, I made the decision to get on board this train to nowhere in the hope of reaching Berlin around 9 a.m. Heading west, then north, then south. I should have been going east, only east.

In broken English, the woman in the ticket office had tried to assure me that by taking three trains through the night, in snow covered Poland and with a temperature of minus six degrees centigrade, I would arrive in Berlin in the morning. She was a sweet old lady who would soon be going to her sweet little home, to eat a bowl of sweet hot soup before jumping in bed with her sweet old man. Did she realise she was sending me on the bitterest of train rides?

In the UK, this journey would have been an impossible concept for a number of reasons, the first and most important being that there were probably no trains operating through the night. And if by some miracle any trains were running, there was not a chance in hell they would be on-time to make such very tight connections. Still, I anyway bought the tickets, not convinced for one second that I would actually have the courage to board the first train.

"I'm sitting in a railway station, got a ticket for my destination." Simon and Garfunkel had me in one.

Five minutes ago, I nearly called it a day. Maja's scrap of paper with her telephone number on it was in my pocket, and her warm bed was more than tempting. But that first train rolled-in and I took a leap of faith, opened a door and entered a corridor. The train pulled away as I finally reached an eight-person compartment. I could hear the noise filling that corridor before I got anywhere near my destination, and I just knew I was going to be joining the party. Fate was being played out for me this night and was making me very astute! Hauling my luggage already had me in a sweat. The train was over-heated to compensate for the freezing night outside. However, looking into my compartment I almost froze.

Inside seven Poles stopped their partying and stared at me. I must have looked like a ghost. One of them had a sneer on his face that spoke a thousand words, it said, 'Are you really going to come in here?' And I did, I went in there; by some unseen force of nature, I squeezed myself into that over-crowded, sauna hot compartment. Me, sweating but freezing in my winter coat, two bags and enough desperation and fatigue to last a lifetime. The past eight hours had seemed like an eternity. Eight hours ago, I was merrily heading to the Belarus border, oblivious of what was about to unfold.

No one spoke to me, but at least they got on with the party. There were crates of beer, enough to get them through the night. I would have died for one. But my wits had long deserted me, so there was no way I was asking for one. Less than an hour ago I had been with a different kind of Pole. I really must have looked so pathetic that they just didn't bother with me. It was as if I didn't exist. I sat there, a quivering wreck for four of the longest hours of my life. I wanted to be back in the minibus with the soldiers.

There is something about young men with no hair that unnerves people. I mean, I have virtually no hair, and I would be amazed if I put the frighteners on anyone. Maybe it's the fact that at their age they choose to cut it all off. Me, I have no choice. Those boys certainly put the frighteners on me for the first minutes in their company.

I was heading to Krzyz. Just the name filled me with despair. Where was it? What did I do when I got there? And how would I know when I reached it? Most important was to stay awake.

Easy, I was too petrified to fall asleep. But the windows were completely steamed up, and even if I could rub a hole through one, there was a blizzard raging outside. We stopped from time to time, but never for too long, and rarely could make out the station names. What I did know, and this proved to be a life saver, was that my next train to Kostrzyn was due to depart at 4:20 a.m. As 4 a.m. approached, I panicked and gathered my last shred of respect, together with my luggage and stood outside a toilet in the passageway, waiting and hoping. The elderly female guard who had checked my ticket earlier sneaked up behind me and tapped me on my shoulder. I nearly jumped out of my skin. Please don't think I am some snivelling coward or the like. I have travelled the planet and encountered some strange situations, but this night was pushing me to my limit. So, was I nervy? You bet your life I was.

She was jabbering on, and I had no idea what she was saying, but the train was slowing, and I caught a glimpse of a station sign KRZ. Her animation made me realise I has being released from this hell. As the train stopped, I almost leapt off onto the platform. Perhaps half a dozen others disembarked with me. Grey ghosts drifting through the snow. Grey and white, a theme that would follow me for the next week or so. I was some kind of a zombie and just followed them. They headed into a station and then straight out onto a platform and boarded another train. I frantically caught up with an old man and shoved my ticket in his face. 'Tak,' he calmly said, as if talking to a stupid child. 'Tak,' and pointed at the train the ghosts were boarding. So, I followed him and obediently joined those ghosts.

Really, where were they going at this time of night? Me, I had a very sound reason, escape, adventure, fear... but where were the ghosts going at four in the morning? Off a-haunting perhaps?

Once on board, I showed three other passengers my ticket. They all nodded, and the third said in the purest queens English, 'Yes sir, this is the train you are booked on.' I nearly kissed him. I collapsed onto a bench. Shivers ran down my spine at the thought that I had nearly missed Krzyz. A name I would never forget, and always recall with a mixture of fear and elation. I was in an open carriage. No claustrophobic compartments, no crates of beer or partying skinheads. I knew they must have been okay, those Polish boys, and I knew that because me and my luggage were here on this train, living proof of the fact.

As I calmed down, a slowly growing respect for the Polish railway system started to develop in my mind. We arrived through all that horrific weather on time. And we departed on time, and finally, we reached Kostrzyn on time. The Poles made the Swiss look like train amateurs.

The journey to Kostrzyn, gratefully proved uneventful, and as I stood on the platform of yet another station waiting for my train to Berlin, I encountered a rare moment of peace at the thought that I would actually arrive at Berlin airport in time to catch the flight Sofia was on, heading to Moscow. Peace, at the fact that in my moment of extreme adversity, I had found a way to overcome the trauma, and get this trip

23

back on track. There was no Passepartout to help me, just a kindly, sweet old lady, who knew a thing or two about the Polish train network. I'm sure Phileas would have quietly cheered my powers of endurance and tenacity. I hadn't slept for more than 24 hours, I had traversed Poland, twice, and yes, I did return to Berlin, and much sooner than I had anticipated.

Am I stoic? I never considered myself so, but after the ordeals of this night! So, on a cold, snowing morning, 29 hours after I had left Berlin, I returned to that wonderful, restored capital city of the new Germany. It had taken six trains and 16 hours since leaving my *friends* in Belarus, but here I was, waiting for a bus to take me to the airport. The final leg of a never to be forgotten night.

It was sometime later that I tried to assess my performance in the theatre production I had found myself in that night. It was *a hard day's night* for sure, but I somehow came through it. I had stayed calm outwardly, whilst inwardly reeling from one situation to another. I wondered if I should have made different choices, but resoundingly I felt that by following my instincts I led myself out of the dark into the light. The Trans-Siberian, Sofia and the need to not let down Phileas had all played a part in bringing me through. I showed a determination to achieve my goals, and that is probably true of me in life, in general. I set myself goals and then follow my instincts to realise them. I felt happy on that bus ride to the airport. And that was something I hadn't expected. I was suddenly light, and yes, happy.

I finally checked in for my flight to Moscow, and upon entering the terminal, headed for a coffee shop, and my first food in 24 hours. My stomach was knotted, and I had to force a cheese sandwich down my throat.

I knew I wasn't in good shape, but it was the look on

Sofia's face that made me realise what a mess I must be. Later she told me she was shocked but tried not to show it. But she did show it, and after a trip to a restroom, I could see why. It would take a few days for me to fully recover, but by then the next drama was already beginning to unfold, and the consequences of it would make my recent suffering feel like a walk in the park.

It was midday and I was in Berlin. By midnight I hoped to be in Moscow, on a train that would carry me across the wilderness of Siberia to Beijing. I was getting back on track, and finally again, heading east.

This was not my first time in Moscow. My previous visit had been a business trip which had involved very little business and a lot of eating cold meat followed by vodka shots. I remembered Moscow as a grey, cold city, and nothing had changed much. Still grey, still cold, although colder now in the midst of winter. I really had to make an effort to visit in the summer months.

But one thing had clearly changed, and that was the unmistakable smell of money. Money... money everywhere. New 4x4 mammoths clogging the streets, and designer stores on every corner. For a state reborn through communism only a century before, I have yet to visit a country with less extremes of rich and poor. The *haves* certainly have a lot, and the *have nots* certainly do not. Perhaps, it was always like that, hence the *revolution* in the first place! All those Tsars and Tsarinas with their Fabergé eggs; who owns those shiny baubles now? Probably the same people who own European football clubs and half of the Côte D'Azur. With such phenomenal resources, surely Russia should make Norway seem third-world. But no, nothing of the sort. Some of those *reds* had quite some roubles under their *beds*, and if the prices we were expected to pay at the Bolshoi Restaurant were anything to go by, they would need them.

As a Russian friend, who I jokingly call Tsarina, once said to me, 'Russia is a fat cow who was lying on her side. The Revolution came and she stood up. She then laid back down on her other side.' That cow was for sure lying down, taking life easy and being milked for every possible rouble.

We planned to leave our luggage at the train station and spend the already dark evening looking around Red Square, then having dinner, before boarding the train. We were dropped at Jaroslavski train station. It was like stepping back in time. I could picture troops heading off to the front with a loaf of bread and a bottle of vodka to send them on their way to the miserable end that awaited them. I mean, some didn't even have rifles.

Phileas booked passage by train to Italy. Perhaps even the *Orient Express* with all its opulent beauty. That was really travelling in style. No short-cuts in that department for Phileas. He may have suffered and endured along the way, but he had a bag full of money to throw around as needed, to ensure he won his bet.

The first glimpse of the *Vostok*, our train across Siberia, was both exciting and concerning. It definitely was not the *Orient Express*. Phileas would not have been amused. But British stiff upper lip forbade me to show any disappointment. Appearances can be deceptive, and this was certainly the case with the *Vostok* because the inside made the outside look wonderful. She was a massive red beast stretching as far as we could see down the never-ending platform in the grey, wet mist that enveloped the station. She was heading to Peking at 11:55 p.m., which left only a few hours to hit the town.

The taxi from the airport had been expensive, but at least luxurious. The clapped-out old excuse for a cab which took us on a 15-minute ride was exorbitant. As the expression goes, *"He saw us coming"*. We rattled along in the stifling heat of the taxi to finally escape into the freezing cold majesty of Red Square. You could stand in the centre and make a 360 degrees whistle-stop tour of Moscow must-sees. Lenin's Mausoleum, St Basil's Cathedral, and the GUM department store, the latter lit up like Harrods in London.

Despite its unquestionable beauty, we had little time for St Basil's and Lenin, time was pressing, and by now I was starving.

Sofia had done her homework and recommended a place for us to eat. The Bolshoi Restaurant was something straight out of the grand old days of Moscow. Roman columns, fancy artwork, and a lot of white. Oh, and most important of all, outrageous prices. I mean, off the scale. But we were seated before we realised that, so no chance of escape. I recall one bottle of something fancy was US $27,000. Sofia looked right at home in her fancy coat and fur hat, I looked like a tramp she had dragged off the street in some overt charitable act to make the oligarchy feel guilty of all their wealth. And some of those elite few were definitely having a good night out at the Bolshoi. They may not have been batting eyelids at the prices, but mine were doing somersaults. The meal could prove more expensive than the combined cost of my journey around the world.

I tried to smile as I assessed my options. Dash for the door, shouting, 'I'm going to miss my train,' or 'My grandmother has been taken sick.' Or perhaps the truth, 'Too expensive, bye.' I think the waiter in his cold but understanding way had already clocked on to the fact that we were just a pair of misinformed poor tourists, as he suddenly appeared with a half-sheet scrap of paper with a special daily menu. It could have been entitled *For the poor and needy*, it was for sure a welcome sight. Yes, the options were limited, but at least I wouldn't have to trade my Trans-Siberian train ticket to eat.

We were able to laugh about the situation at the time, and often afterwards. We ordered the cheapest items on that menu, and a glass each of the cheapest house wine. When the bill came, I still felt as if I was being skinned. It made the taxi fares look reasonable. We left into chill night air and sought out a ride back to the station with a mixture of relief and awe. Awe that later we could at least boast we had eaten at one of the most expensive restaurants on the planet!

Arriving back at Jaroslavski train station, we collected our luggage and headed for the Vostok. She was still sitting there, as if frozen to the tracks. I would later learn that such a thing was possible.

Climbing aboard carriage number 4, Moscow to Peking, clearly the Russian Train Authority were not aware there had been a name change. We were greeted by our *provodnitsa* Leaena, who showed us to our compartment, number 2.

We were ready to say *dasvidaniya* to Moscow, and I remember thinking I wouldn't be in a hurry to return unless I struck lucky on the Lotto.

At five minutes before midnight exactly we felt a jolt, and whistles rang out, as we slowly moved forward to start our long-haul to Beijing. I was heading east again. My soldier and skinhead friends were being left behind me in the west as I progressed east into the unending white and grey of *Mother Russia*.

I know I should have been elated, even excited, at the prospect of what lay ahead, but the past couple of days had left me with a feeling of unease. And now, travelling with a companion, I felt less empowered to make my own decisions. So, the opposite was true, I felt ill at ease and nervous, and a few days later those feelings would sure prove to be justified.

Day 5 Trans-Siberian Railway

In which the beauty of the journey is all that matters

"Anything one man can imagine, other men can make real." - Jules Verne

I awoke to snow. Snow and the endless white tundra of Siberia would be my partner for the coming days. Along with Sofia. And she was going to cause me some troubles. But my woes would be incomparable to hers.

Only four days had passed since leaving London, but it felt like weeks ago since I departed St. Pancras on the *Eurostar*. My flirting with adventure had taken some unexpected turns. It left me wondering how 60 plus days would feel.

To be very clear, I do not consider myself a romantic, so quite why I carried Christmas decorations in my luggage, to put up in our carriage, I will never know. But that's what I did and found myself doing after waking on our first morning on the *Vostok*.

Shortly after leaving Moscow the previous night, we took stock of how life would unfold on the journey across Siberia. To her credit, Sofia put on a brave face. For me, anything was better than the compartment I had shared with the skinheads, so I probably was not so disappointed, although I would have had every right to be so.

Omar Sharif and Julie Christie had no reason to complain at train conditions; they were in the middle of one of the greatest revolutions in history. But we were living in the 21st century and expected a little more comfort - not luxury, just comfort - after all, we were travelling first class! Our compartment was small. Very small. There was no bathroom, at least no bath or shower. Just stainless-steel toilets and basins. And we would be sharing those wonderful facilities with the rest of the carriage. We would be on this train for a week, so hygiene was clearly going to be an issue. This was not *glamping*, this was *tramping*. Well, that's what I jokingly called it, camping on a train! Sofia didn't get the joke. Well, she is Italian, so perhaps it was that, or perhaps the lack of facilities had deadened her humour.

I realise I may sound a little negative about the *Vostok*, also numbered 20. Only the prestigious trains in Russia are given names, so the Vostok was a *somebody*. I had travelled on trains from the U.K. to Belarus, and in comparison, the *Vostok* was an equal. I guess the issue was that we would be staying on it for a week, not just a couple of nights. Taking *sleepers* across China and the U.S. later on this journey, I would be able to better form an opinion and comparison.

The previous night I hadn't slept at all, so even though I was on some kind of nervous high, I slept like a log. My body and mind simply gave in to all that had gone before and collapsed. It did me good, that sleep. I woke refreshed and ready to enjoy the coming days in a peaceful state. Ready to shake off the Belarus Blues, get my mojo back, and get back on track.

Sofia hadn't slept so well, but was in good spirits, and I think the combination of the sweetness of my Christmas decorations, and simple determination to buckle down and get on with things added to that. We started our day and journey on an upper.

Maybe it was a premonition, maybe she was just being thoughtful, or the fact that she needed to eat some of her own food. Whatever the reason, Sofia, like a magician with a white rabbit, produced an enormous wedge of parmigiana cheese, prosciutto, salami and Italian coffee from her bag. If it wasn't a premonition, it should have been, because what we would find in the dining car that evening would have us gorging on her supplies for the next couple of days.

Trains travelling across Mother Russia have a samovar, and it proved a life saver. *"I don't take coffee, I take tea, my dear."* The Englishman had brought tea, Earl Grey, and the Italian woman, coffee. Whatever else may occur, hot drinks would not be an issue. But that samovar, with its steaming hot water, would be called upon for the endless pots of noodles we would buy at the stations along the route. And let me say, it was a magnificent specimen, that samovar. Tsar Nicholas would have approved being served from it.

Our *provonitsa and provodnik* popped in to say hello. Neither Leaena nor Andre spoke a word of any language other than their mother tongue. Although a few days later, when demanding we leave the train in the middle of Siberia, Andre did make himself very clear!

At midday, we made our first stop at a place called Kirov. Along the route the train line had given rise to towns and villages. This was our first experience of station and platform life, and it pretty much shaped the coming days. Descending the few steps, I heard a loud metallic banging. Leaena was striking an ice-covered metal pipe hanging down from the train, with an axe. She was stocky, let's say, solidly built. Perhaps in her fifties and looked to be twice the man that Andre was. That's probably why she did the heavy duties. As I soon discovered, also the shitty duties. She was hammering the ice and other materials from the toilet waste pipe that off-loaded directly onto the tracks. Yes, it was cold. And that pipe froze quickly, so I guess to avoid a backlog of our parmigiana, the pipe needed to be clattered at every station we stopped at.

Leaena was quite a sight. She was dressed in a fur hat

with her flowing blond locks hanging down on the shoulders of her beautiful blue coat; her outfit finished off with fur lined boots. I noticed she had applied a bright red lipstick before reaching Kirov. She prepared herself for the stops. Holding her massive axe, reversed to use as a hammer, she was not a woman to be messed with.

This stop also afforded us the chance to see who else was mad enough to be travelling across this wilderness in the middle of winter. And there were not that many of us, or perhaps the other passengers knew the routine and decided to stay on board. Either way, a few stragglers, and us tourists, took to the platform. Our first stop brought shared excitement. Later stops I would experience on my own.

I wasn't sure what century I was in, let alone decade. Old women in multiple layers of clothing carrying baskets of dried fish, bread and other home-produced goodies surrounded us. Those *babushkas* were also selling homemade vodka in clear bottles. Sofia bought some fish and bread, but we resisted the *hootsch*. We later learnt from a reasonably good source that the vodka was of highly questionable quality. Something about bringing on blindness made us thankful we resisted.

The platform had a kiosk. It was well stocked, but two items jumped out at me. Pots of noodles and chocolate. Many years of living on my own had taught me the value of these goodies. I bought a reasonable supply of both. Being an artist, the chocolate wrapper appealed to me. A chubby little girl wrapped in a green scarf. She wasn't smiling, that little girl, and after trying some of her chocolate, I understood why. The chocolate was not quite up to Swiss or Belgian standards. I still have that chocolate paper wrapper with that unsmiling little girl, a reminder, perhaps, to appreciate the better things in life.

Laden with our supplies, we re-boarded the Vostok and were soon on our way back *"Into the Wild"*.

The view from the window is a succession of endless fields and forests interspersed by the odd village or hamlet. All is white. The window is like a television showing your favourite show. Try as I may to read or study, I was drawn back to the window. I lost myself in the views. We played backgammon, we talked, and reflected on life. There is no daily news to consume us, only the past and the present. The day, as will many ahead of us, drifts on in calmness. It feels like nothing can break this idyll. Yes, we are a little cramped, and there is nothing to excite us on the train, but the views are majestic, and the rhythm of the train is invading us. It soaks in and leaves a stain. When I experience moments in my life such as these, they stay with me. They help form who I am, and who I will be. Travelling, more than any other experience, does this to me. The simply *being* in this moment, at this time, and never to live it again.

In the afternoon we stop again, this time at Balyezino. Do the names matter? I would never remember them without reference to my journal. Some stick though, some are never to be forgotten. Krzyz, in Poland; I'll never forget that name, or that place, or that experience. The ghosts of Krzyz will always haunt me.

I wandered down the platform passing the freight carriages, finally reaching the enormous electric engine that was pulling our kilometre-long train. It was red with bright orange horizontal stripes. I guess they were there to be seen in the snow, not that it could have slowed down very quickly in an emergency. I had only thought of the carrying of passengers; but I was watching a lot of cargo loading and unloading.

The Trans-Siberian is the longest railway in the world at just over 9000 kilometres. Without it, modern Russia would be a very different place. Respect where it is due, the Trans-Siberian had evolved Russian history, in a similar way to the railways that forged their way across the prairies to the west coast of America. All in all, trains deserved a better rap.

Afternoon turned to evening and with it the prospect of a decent meal. I had read a quote about travelling on the Trans-Siberian *"First, second and third class are all available on-board along with a comfortable dining car with an extensive selection of culinary delights."* I must admit I was excited to visit the dining car. I hadn't had a full proper *culinary delight* since leaving England. Mostly I had lived on snacks and sausages. So, I carried a heavy expectation into that dining car, and I can honestly say, I left it there.

There had been a few people on the platforms so I assumed the dining-car would be full. Those other passengers obviously knew something I didn't. There was only one occupied table, and clearly our dining companions were tourists. In fact, two middle-aged Koreans and their Russian guide. The menu looked promising, and we ordered beers, borsch and a beef dish. Total €20, for that I could barely get bread and water at the Bolshoi Restaurant. It's fair to say the meal was not a massive success. The food was less than average, and there wasn't a culinary delight in sight.

Unbeknown to me, the evening was going to take a bad turn, as I said something to Sofia to upset her. For the record, I do not intend to purposely upset people, and I didn't remember saying anything that evening, but a few years later, laughing over that meal, she told me what I said, and it simply didn't register with me. I'll put it down to my anxiety hangover from Poland rather than insensitivity.

I'm not sure what the consequence of my words were on her, but I reflect that they may have set a tone for the coming days, and if so, I feel mighty guilty because I hold a dear place for her in my heart. Sticks and stones may break your bones, but words *will* kill you!

We agreed to give the supposed culinary delights another try tomorrow, and if no improvement, we would pass and stick to noodles. With that, we settled into a movie on Sofia's laptop, then called it a night. Our first full day on the rails, had nearly come off them, but we pulled ourselves back on track for the days ahead. Little did we know we would be derailed so soon, and so dramatically.

Day 6 Trans-Siberian

Where station life proves to be an entertainment all of its own, and an appreciation of Vodka is acquired

"Trains are wonderful. To travel by train is to see nature and human beings, towns and churches and rivers, in fact, to see life." - Agatha Christie

I slept like there was no tomorrow. My body simply gave in to the exhaustion of the previous days and said, 'That's enough.' Consequently, I woke refreshed and feeling great. My positive mood heightened by the sight before my eyes; the grey of Moscow replaced with clear blue skies and the sun shining down in all its winter glory on the snow-covered countryside. A window on Siberia, and one to melt any heart.

Breakfast of cheese, bread, tea and coffee and we were set up for our first stop, Tyumen. Now understanding the food situation, we topped up our supplies from the station kiosks and *babushkas*. We risked a dark brown loaf and smoked fish, which out here could only have come from a lake or river. Our expectations were not high, but, hey ho, we decided to give it a try. With six days still to go, we wanted to broaden our diet, and Sofia's supplies would not last for ever.

It's funny what images stay with you. On the platform I saw a stray dog that looked more like a jackal, eating some food dropped by the old ladies. He, protective of his find, looked up at me, with a 'Don't even think about it' look. I had no attention of doing anything of the kind. Perhaps he didn't get to see many foreigners, and realise we feed our dogs.

I stood between two carriages and timidly placing a

foot on each plate, I looked down into the snowy gap to the tracks and thought that slipping would not be a good idea, as I would have to hop my way round the world! But that gap immediately transported me back to Berlin. Images like music and smells will do that. I was standing on the line between west and east. I had now well and truly crossed that divide. I was definitely in the east and heading further into it. The *Iron Curtain* may be long gone, but its legacy remained and entering Moscow a couple of days before made me feel its presence. Actually, the Belarusians had done a pretty good job of making me understand that pan-European harmony had not yet been fully achieved. Is Russia even in Europe? I mean it reaches to Alaska. It turns out that most of the population live in Europe, and most of the land mass is in Asia!

Sofia was in great spirits despite the sanitary arrangements. She was putting on one hell of a brave face, because she looked radiant. She had gone for the Tsarina look and pulled it off; fur lined boots and coat, topped off with a spectacular mauve fur hat. She could grace any *Vogue* cover. Me, I looked like a tramp next to her, a real-life Lady and the Tramp situation. If there had been anyone to notice, they would certainly have thought, 'What's she doing with him?' - I mean, even I was thinking it! When she descended to the platform at our stops, it was like a scene from a movie. So much grey filled by a flash of stardust.

The station stops were a highlight. Sometimes we had time to explore a little further, even out of the station. No one ever asked about tickets, or where we were going. I guess out here a foreigner wouldn't be trying to skip a fare. If you got off the train, you would for sure to be getting back on it. At Omsk, we had time to take a good look around. I found an English-speaking local to chat to in the station, who took the occasion of our meeting to complain that the Russian government had not built a metro system in Omsk; which being a city with a population over one million, was policy. I thought about that, and back to a previous visit I made to Moscow, when I had taken refuge from the cold in the metro. And there was a whole other world going on down there under the ice and snow. So perhaps the people of Omsk had a case. Not that sounding off to me was going to change anything. Anyhow I showed sympathy and made a note to take it up the next time I attended a *Politburo* meeting.

Omsk station was an amazing shade of pale blue and could have got lost in the sky from a distance. Alarmingly I noted the temperature was minus 26 degrees centigrade. The quicker they built the metro for the good folks in Omsk, the better. My nasal hairs, I only have a few, froze - and my beard wasn't too happy. Needless to say, we didn't hang around outside for very long.

It was a shame we didn't have longer at some of the stops to explore. Omsk had quite some culture and places of interest, with art galleries, a theatre and cathedral. The only way to spend more time was to leave the train and re-board another - this meant over-night stays and delays, and time was not on our side. After all, I was a traveller not a tourist, my clock was ticking all the way back to London.

Re-entering the station, I notice Comrade Lenin staring down at me. He would pop up numerous times along the track. We got back to the train just in time. It made me wonder if they would have left without us. Would Andre or Leaena have raised the alarm? Something told me not. This massive snake wasn't going to be held up by a couple of missing westerners. We departed at 2:10 p.m. as the sun was setting. The impact of remaining on Moscow time was beginning to take its toll, with ever shortening daylight.

The fish proved to be perch, and was more fat than meat, and with very little taste. Another option crossed off the list. The noodles would prove a bigger lifesaver than I had initially thought. I was drinking a local beer, surprisingly named *Windmill*, as we pulled into Barabinsk, with a further drop in temperature.

That evening, and in desperation, we decided to give the dining car another shot. Our new and only fellow travellers, the Koreans, were already there. They probably had a better appreciation of the local fare than we did. Or perhaps it was the vodka, ever present on their table that was numbing their taste buds. Their guide offered us a couple of shots, and I have to say that until that day I steered away from vodka. It was my day of initiation, and I became a convert. We were told not to buy the moonshine from the *babushkas*, and only drink *Russian Standard* or *Beluga*. Their offer was the former, and during the journey I tried both. *Russian Standard* has been my choice ever since, and I in turn have converted a few people to this smooth liquor. Smooth, very smooth; no mixer required, just stick the bottle in the freezer.

Dinner didn't hold any positive surprises, so it was our last attempt before entering China. We would have to be more creative in our search at the stations we visited along the way, as our Italian supplies were fast diminishing. The stress of reaching Moscow had definitely shed a few kilos, and at this rate I would achieve (hoped for) weight loss before arriving in Hong Kong!

A final stop for the evening was Novosibirsk, another city that wouldn't exist but for the arrival of the railway.

The station was a grand structure, with chandeliers filling the waiting room. As we pulled away, two enormous statues of a family were waving us farewell. They were actually waving farewell to the brave comrade soldiers off to fight the invading Germans. Alas more than 20 million of those comrades never returned home!

They looked happy enough, the family, with rolled up shirt sleeves and summer clothes. When would it ever be warm enough for shirtsleeves? With the temperature now dropping into the minus thirties, summer would be a long time coming. The people choosing to live out here must be pretty hardy. Good boots would definitely be essential. More than 30 minutes off the train would confirm that mine were totally inadequate.

Day 7 Trans-Siberian

In which nothing much happens that didn't happen yesterday

"Even in Siberia there is happiness." - Anton Chekhov

Before we had time to eat breakfast, we had an early morning stop at Krasnoyarsk. Waking at 6am to gleaming sunshine in the middle of winter is disconcerting. I really wonder how people living close to the Arctic Circle cope with the extremes.

Wandering the platform, I checked out two trains waiting at the station. Both were headed to Vladivostok, and both were crammed full of people, many on triple bunks. That meant six people to a compartment. Our compartment was certainly not the height of luxury, but this was something else altogether. Remind me to never travel third class in Russia.

I guess the train was cheaper than flying, but it was a hell of a long way to endure those conditions. Although maybe I had it all wrong, and they were having a ball of a time, playing cards, and partying perhaps. My instincts told me otherwise.

Krasnoyarsk must be some kind of summer getaway, as there were many thousands of small summer houses, *dachas*. Chekhov rated it the most beautiful city in Siberia, and he certainly knew a thing or two about beauty. Again, I felt the urge to get off the train and stay awhile. I may have to seriously consider a return to Siberia, and perhaps in the summer months, although isn't the place swarming with mosquitos? Well at least it was in *The Way Back*, when the gulag escapees were fleeing across this vast land.

Those *dachas* are a cross between Swiss chalets and English beach huts. Mostly wooden with steep roofs; presumably to let the snow fall off in winter. Colourful little boxes waiting to receive their own escapees. And half the Russian population owns one, so escaping would appear to be very popular!

We roll on through the Urals, once again breakfasting on cheese and salami. I love parmigiana, but I have my limits! I switch to noodles and chocolate for lunch, and those little beauties I will never be bored with.

Back to the restroom situation. As if keeping clean wasn't hard enough, the tap over the basin had to be lifted to release water. This means that you cannot run the water, so effectively you are washing one handed as the basin doesn't have a plug. What genius thought this was a smart idea? Maybe it's a way of conserving water, otherwise any other reason is simply bonkers; I'm sure most prisons have better restroom facilities. Clever as she is, Sofia brought with her a large supply of wet wipes.

The toilet releases directly onto the tracks. I thought that only happened in India! Needless to say, when we are in a station the restrooms are locked.

To wash our cups, plates and cutlery we use Leaena's little sink in her operations room. She finds this highly amusing; I'm pleased one of us does. I may sound a little grumpy on this subject, and perhaps in general. I would say at that time I was not, but now a few years later, I'm definitely turning into a grumpy old man. Maybe it's something we can only develop with age. We need to have lived through *stuff* and people, to realise how annoying it can all be. Anyway, I like being grumpy, it nearly always puts a smile on my face.

The operation room is sweet. One small sink, one small chair and one chubby *provodnitsa*. Stainless steel abounds. I wonder where, when, and if she and Andre sleep. The idea, I voice to Sofia, that it could be together, makes us both laugh out loud. Other than hammering on and clearing the poo tube when we reach a station, I haven't seen either of them do any work.

As for our cabin, let's say it has limitations. There are no two pin sockets, so charging telephones and computers is done in the passageway. There is a central light and four reading lights. There is a television, but it doesn't work. The two bunks are small but comfortable with sheets and blankets. A small table, which half folds onto the other half, which has proved very useful for our backgammon games, and putting Sofia's computer on to watch movies. Surprisingly, there is a rug, along with another outside our compartment door in the passageway, presumably placed so we can trip over it, which I do regularly.

We were two in what may be a four-berth cabin. With four it would be more than cosy. There is ample luggage space, but ordinarily you wouldn't need much luggage, as you probably will not be dressing for dinner.

The temperature is maintained at 24 degrees centigrade, day and night, so there is about a 50-degree variance to outside, and boy does it hit you like an express train when you venture out, excuse the pun.

The afternoon passes into night, although since 3 p.m. it's been pitch black outside. Undisturbed by stops, we settle down to chat, games and movies. I couldn't pick a better travelling companion, except none at all. Sofia is great, the difficult is made easy, and the easy made fun. Never a dull moment, and always something to talk about. But stormy waters are not far over the horizon, and our calm passage will give way to a very rough ride and push our patience to its limit.

Travel Tip: If you are thinking to take this journey, I suggest you bring the following: food and drink, crockery and cutlery, a two-pin extension cable, a computer or pad with entertainment, wet wipes, soap, towel, relaxing and ultra-warm clothing. Whatever you do, book first class!

Day 8 Trans-Siberian, Lake Baikal

In which a battle rages between the tenacious and obstinate

"In the middle of Siberia I guess there's a lake that big (like the Great Lakes), but there are practically no other lakes that big with fresh water." - Kurt Vonnegut

At some point, early morning, I realised Sofia was ill. The next day I returned from the washroom to find her walking down the carriage in her underwear. I mean, it was minus 30 degrees centigrade outside. Clearly, she had a problem, and that problem was to get worse. Why was reaching Hong Kong proving so difficult?

Sometime during the night, we reached Lake Baikal, the world's largest freshwater lake, and caught a glimpse of it waking at 6 a.m. Time was a big issue on the Trans-Siberian.

At that moment, the lake was a beautiful vast swathe of blue under clear skies, surrounded by crisp snows. Amazingly, I discovered there are freshwater seals (aptly named the Baikal Seal) inhabiting the lake. Seals sure do like the cold - I would encounter a great many of them having fun in Antarctica a few years later - although those ball balancing pinnipeds are much larger than their little brothers in the lake. That respite from the grey was welcomed but short lived, as the grey, heavily laden skies were soon to return. And with that returning heaviness, the weight of a clearly sick travelling companion. Sofia had all the symptoms of a suddenly arrived virus; fever, headache, aching body - if it existed, she had it. And where were we? Halfway across Siberia in *no man's land*, and one of us had a schedule to keep. As the day wore on so did this malaise increase, as Sofia refused to communicate about her condition. Firstly, I just thought she was having an *off day*, but morning passed into afternoon, and she wasn't drinking, eating or saying much. Later I understood she didn't want to burden me with her problem; however, this was exactly what was causing me difficulty. I was in the dark as to what was going on.

Sofia can be obstinate and contrary. I have a love/hate relationship with her qualities. We are all different, and all have our *issues*. But right now, I wasn't seeing any positives; I wanted to throttle her, then comfort her, and most of all get rid of her. It may sound harsh, but I couldn't get her to explain her condition. Very frustrating. I wasn't mentally in such a good place either. I was a mixture of emotions, and a little lost. I think Belarus was beginning to crowd in on me, like aftershock. Phileas was traveling with Passepartout and finally an Indian princess; I was accompanied by a mute tetchy Tsarina. I love her dearly, but not right at that moment. A lesson to learn, about attempting this *Wacky Race* against time, go solo.

Another thing to say about Phileas is that he was always so cool. In the movie they cleverly cast David Niven, so British *stiff upper lip*, and calm determination. I was showing signs of cracking up. I would need to kick back a little and find a few quiet days away from this madness. In those hours of solitude, wrapped in my own mind, and Sofia silently attending to her situation. I looked for reasons for this feeling of disquiet within me. Was it the trains? Too many trains, trapped in small compartments, perhaps a little claustrophobic. Just wait until I would board those cargo ships, then I would know what claustrophobia was... what joys still to come! Too much unanticipated stress. Poor preparation, and that on all levels. Or was this all just a stupid idea, which I shouldn't have even begun to entertain. This trip of fantasy. Just over a week had passed, and there was a great deal stretching ahead of me, and most of it into the unknown. I'm a rational, pragmatic sort of man, but the cracks were beginning to show, and I had nothing to fill them with, other than hope. As Andy Dufresne says in the *Shawshank Redemption*, *"Hope is a good thing, maybe the best of the things. And no good thing ever dies."* Good old Andy, I think about that quote often. And right then I was hoping. Hoping for Sofia to get well, and the sun to shine, and some decent food, and eight hours of sleep, a shower, not too much really in the scheme of things.

Time passed slowly on that train, and time was an issue. It was all mixed up. For most of the duration of the journey from Moscow until the Chinese border the clocks were fixed at Moscow time. This irrespective of how many time zones we went through. East, and further east, but still on Moscow time. So, waking at 8 a.m. gave us three to five hours of daylight, if we were lucky. By 2 p.m. it was already dark. There are 11 time-zones in Russia, and on reaching Lake Baikal we were on Moscow time plus five of them. My body clock was having kittens, not knowing when to sleep, eat or anything else. Jack Reacher has a built-in clock to within minutes, if you believe Lee Child, but I defy Jack to sort out this mess.

In fairness to Sofia, none of this could have helped her condition. Eating poorly, not sleeping, no reasonable sanitary conditions, and worst of all, me. I'm sure there were times when she wanted to kill me! But she put on a brave face, suffering silently and with dignity. Oh, what I would give to have a fraction of her dignity. And let me make it clear, since trundling through the wilderness of Siberia together, we have often been able to reflect and laugh about that trip, and marvel in the madness of it all and our restraint to *not* kill each other. Always loving each other in the deepest of ways, and always staying the best of friends. But then, with my increasingly shredded nervousness at what was coming next, there were times when I would have switched that Russian train carriage for the one which took me through the night across Poland, finally off-loading me in Krzyz. And that really *is* saying something!

We finally reached Ulan Ude where the track divides. Right turn takes the Trans-Siberian railway through Mongolia, and left continues through Russia, both eventually reaching Beijing. With time pressing I opted for the Russian route, later dividing again between Vladivostok and Beijing at Chita.

The *Vostok* continued stopping every few hours at stations along the route. I always disembarked. Sometimes having only a matter of minutes before the blaring horn demanding re-boarding sounded, others with an hour or so to explore further afield from the station. Some things never changed, like the weather, always cold and snowy, and the trackside smells of oil, and station heat. So hot and always full of people, some travellers, some perhaps escaping the cold and taking refuge, the stations were a continual source of surprise. At Ulan Ude I found an optician whose eye-test card displayed pictures of animals, in decreasing sizes. I guessed reading, and education in general, could be limited out here in this *nowhere* land. Before making this journey, I assumed there was nothing out here, in Siberia, but I was wrong. It is the size of the U.S.A., with a population of around 30 million. It's vast, but it's not empty. The largest population centres follow the track, and it was the railway that enabled colonisation of these lands. Who was there to colonise? Local tribes: some I was told still live in their own communities, speaking their own language. What a bleak existence in this grey and cold world, although seeing what civilisation was evolving into with its mega-cities and overcrowding, perhaps following a life in these remote *Sleeping Lands*, as they are called, had its appeal.

What I knew about Siberia before arriving was very little, but I knew it was wealthy. Full of oil, gas, coal and minerals. Didn't those oligarchs owe their riches to these lands, affording them the opportunity to buy their playthings, super yachts and penthouses? I never saw any of their sort wandering the stations of the Trans-Siberian, only working-class souls sheltering from the cold. It was hard to believe these frozen barren lands were really fields of gold. The Russian bear could only growl because of the feed it took from Siberia. What I saw, stopping along this route, through the wilderness, gave no indication of what lay beneath, and what riches it could bring. I saw people, hardly ever smiling, and never friendly. By the same token, never rude or offensive. They were not *happy people*. If anything, it was as though they didn't notice we were even there. During the week on that train and station hopping, I only ever saw two other foreigners, the two Koreans, our dining buddies early in the trip.

A temperature digital display showed minus 32 degrees centigrade as I disembarked at Khilok. It was not my imagination; it *was* getting colder. By now, Sofia, in her delirium, had left me to venture out on my own. I had taken winter clothing, but nothing had prepared me for this. It made Terespol feel springlike. I packed for all climates and throughout this journey round the world I would see a temperature variance of more than 60 degrees. I was at one extreme and couldn't wait to reach the other. I didn't know it then, but Mexico City proved to be the other.

Enough was enough; finally, the *time* issue got to me. I adjusted my watch and phone to Beijing time. I figured it was like setting your time to your destination when flying, it might help any jet lag. I didn't have jet lag, I had train-lag, made worse by food-lag, drink-lag, and sleep-lag. But the good news was that Andre, the *provodnik*, had told me the dining carriage would change at the border the next day to a Chinese one. Finally, sweet and sour prawns, spring rolls and crispy aromatic duck were within touching distance. Not for the first time I would find my expectations would prove exaggerated. Phileas Fogg said, *"There's no such thing as the unexpected."* And perhaps to a smart gentleman such as Phileas that's true, however is it really expecting too much to be able to eat, even average quality food, on a week-long train journey? Throughout Jules Verne's book, we never learn how Phileas, Passepartout and Princess Aouda were catered for on their travels, but I'm sure they would not have been happy if they had to endure my dining car! It was hardly the poached fish, steak and gooseberry pie Phileas was used to at the Reform Club!

Day 9 Trans-Siberian into China

In which crossing into China brings new ordeals for Sofia

"I have found out that there ain't no surer way to find out whether you like people or hate them than to travel with them." - Mark Twain

Another day, another hurdle to jump. Two days to go before journey's end, and things were going from bad to worse. Sofia is in a terrible state. My nerves are getting frazzled again after such a very short respite.

As I returned from the restroom very early in the morning, she was walking towards me down the passageway in her underwear. Asking where she was going was pointless, she was completely out of her mind, and would have had no idea. I guess she saw me missing, and in her delirium came to find me. I corralled her back to the compartment, but not before Andre had witnessed the scene and realised something was drastically wrong.

He came to see me with the Koreans' guide and told me it would be a good idea to take Sofia off the train at the next station. I guess he didn't want a passenger, and especially a foreigner, conking out on his watch - he could end up in one of those lovely Siberian gulags. Obviously, it was not a suggestion that appealed to me. I didn't know where we were, and if we did disembark, when would we be able to catch another train and finish our journey. I tried to speak with Sofia regarding Andre's brainwave. I could have spoken to Leaena's axe for all the good it did me.

The first station stop came and Andre came with it. I made it clear I needed time to think. I was getting no help in that department from Sofia, so I would need to make the call on *Shall we stay, or shall we go now?* Because if we go, *there will be trouble.* She was very ill, and not eating or drinking - on the other hand she was sleeping. I bullied her into taking paracetamol and sips of water from time to time. Finally, I decided we would stay on board. The alternative was too scary.

I would like to think my decision was purely taking Sofia's best interests into account, but selfishly I knew I was also looking out for myself. Not so much the time pressures of keeping up with Phileas, but if we got stuck in Siberia, we would then need to extricate ourselves. What if this took days, or weeks? No, getting off the train presented more problems than it solved.

Later, Sofia thanked me. For her it was critical that she returned to Milan when we reached Beijing. She was in no fit state to decide anything. Honestly, it was one of the hardest decisions I have ever had to make. She was ill, and my responsibility, and it was a heavy one. Now we laugh about the situation, at the time it was pretty scary.

I made it clear we were staying onboard, and Andre just shrugged his shoulders, as if to say, it was all down to me. And it was. I don't blame him or Leaena for washing their hands of this situation. Their view was we had to leave the train, but they couldn't force us.

The rest of the day, and following day were a nightmare. We arrived at the Russia/China border of Zabaikalsk/Manzhouli at midday and the situation took a savage turn. The rolling stock of the train had to be changed to enable the train to operate on the Chinese track, which was a different gauge. This change took three hours, so quite why we had to wait a further five was a mystery. Russian immigration was relatively quick, unlike their Chinese counterparts, which took a further six hours, thus bringing the transfer from The Bear to The Dragon to 14 hours in total.

At the Chinese immigration, they insisted that Sofia and I separately leave the train and attend to our passport check. I decided to go first to suss out the situation, given Sofia's condition. I was escorted into a large hall, remarkably like the one during my short but eventful stay in Belarus. But this time, my visa being in order, I was through in no time. Back at the train, I asked if I could accompany Sofia. A big fat 'NO.' I was nervous, as she could barely speak. My mind was racing at all the possibilities of what could go wrong. Would they think she had swine or bird flu? Perhaps they would assume that a mad woman was trying to enter their country. What I know is, she wasn't through in a jiffy - over an hour later and still no sign of her. Perhaps another hour passed before she appeared, ghost-like and seemingly oblivious to most of what delayed her. I came to understand her passport had got wet from a water bottle in her bag, and some of the ink had smudged. This had led to some intense discussions in the immigration hall, which finally resulted in them deciding to stamp her in. I hate to think what really went down in that immigration hall.

She dejectedly sat and tried to tell me what happened. My heart went out to her. Really! There was so little I could do for her, and yet she was so dependent on me. Eating was out of the question, but I could force some water down her, followed by more paracetamol. I would have died from boredom if I hadn't been a nervous quivering wreck. Come on man, hold it together! I knew I was, but by the thinnest of threads.

Finally, after those unending 14 hours we rolled into the People's Republic of China. I felt neither joy nor relief, just numbness. Sofia felt nothing as she was floating around with the cuckoos.

My body had completely lost track of time. I had no idea if it was morning, afternoon or evening. Times were changing and I had lost track. From the sheer mental exhaustion of it all, I slept like the dead.

Day 10 China

Where the hope of an improved dining experience proves to be a false dawn

"This train of thought was heading straight for Pity City, and she wanted to get off." - Lauren Kate

When you've been down in hell, there is only one way to go: up. We, yes, it is Sofia with the illness, but I've been suffering with her, *really,* so yes, we had been down in that horrible place, and were struggling to find our way up. Hopefully, today would see some improvement in her condition. Certainly, by tomorrow, we needed a change in fortune, as early tomorrow morning we will arrive in Beijing.

We woke up in China, my second superpower of the trip, and if what we saw from the train window was anything to go by, Charles de Gaulle was on the money when he said, *"China is a big country, inhabited by many Chinese."* There is a reason world leaders get the top jobs.

This country was bigger than big, but not as big as Russia. Unlike Russia with vast swathes of countryside, tundra and nothingness, it looked like every inch of China was busy doing something. Mostly trying to feed itself and make money.

Yesterday's dilemma had passed. It had been binary, a hospital in Siberia or one in Beijing. I'd opted, with Sofia's silenced nod of agreement, for Beijing. I think she didn't really understand too much, but what was clearly a fixation was to reach Beijing and the prospect of escaping me. I think at that time she hated me; I was after all the badgering nuisance who was trying to save her life - well that's how I saw it.

By midday she was over the delirium of the previous

evening, but her headache remained, and she wouldn't eat. She kept saying she had to go to work on Monday. There was a fat chance of that happening. What puzzled me was what had caused her condition. We had eaten and drunk the same. I put it down to stress, but if that were the cause, surely, I should be the one suffering, because of the traumas I had experienced before reaching Moscow. They were as stressful as it gets! Although my dramas had not yet passed on my journey around the world, as a run in with the military befell me on driving across the third superpower.

I felt every emotion possible towards Sofia, but the over-riding one was pity, for the terrible state she was in, and my helplessness to aid her. What started as a wonderful journey together had turned into a living nightmare. But her demons were fading, just a little, but that little gave me hope.

Travelling always opens the mind to the spectre of illness, and over the years I've had my fair share of scares. Normally help is readily at hand, but out there in Siberia, all options were less than appealing. For my ocean crossings, the shipping lines involved had insisted on my undergoing health checks and getting some inoculations. I would have 31 days at sea, with limited medical facilities, so the last thing one of those multi-million-dollar ships wanted to do was divert because their solitary passenger decided to get appendicitis, As it happens, I've had mine out, but you get my drift. I was in peak condition before leaving London, perhaps a little less so now, certainly mentally!

Everywhere I looked, China was busy at work. Infrastructure projects abounded along the route. In Russia I had seen very little in the way of development. I guess the oligarchs and government there had other ways to spend their wealth. The Chinese, on the other hand, were all about growth. Two superpowers sharing a common political doctrine, but implementing it is opposing ways. China industrious, Russia laden with resources. Sounds like a recipe for war.

I saw a cow and a stray dog, the first animals for some days now. Where was all the wildlife? Certainly not hugging the railway tracks.

The Chinese dining car should have lifted our spirits after the hiatus of *culinary delights* available on its Russian equivalent. We went along for some lunch, only to discover we had gone from bad to worse. Totally inedible fried rice. How can anyone cock-up rice? And these were Chinese chefs! The idea of rice had raised hopes that Sofia may be able to stomach something; the reality was that today nothing was passing into her other than water.

The train's precision was impressive, and an equal to Poland's. We arrived at each station on time. The day passed slowly, and mostly in silence. There was a great deal to reflect on. My thoughts were to the whole experience of the Trans-Siberian Railway. It was not a trip for comfort or glamour seekers, nor connoisseurs of fine dining. Hercule Poirot would not have been amused. But it offered a unique experience, and one I would always be thankful for.

I guess I may never return to Siberia, but with what looked like some interesting towns and cities along the track, it was always a possibility.

Tomorrow we would arrive in Beijing, and I would hopefully be finding some medical attention for Sofia, and with a large dollop of luck, putting her on a flight home. I was to make my way to Shanghai - the next city on my to-do list. I would be travelling solo for the remainder of my dash around the world, and this prospect did fill with a little comfort. I consider myself a

caring sort of person, but if I had to face adversity, and
I had already faced my fair share, I'd rather do it alone.

Day 11 Beijing to Shanghai

Where upon arriving in Beijing, the first destination of the desperate two, is a hospital

"Someday this war's gonna end." - Lieutenant Colonel Bill Kilgore, Apocalypse Now.

For three days we had been waging war, Sofia and me. Not an intentional war, but one, like so many, born out of misunderstanding and ignorance. It felt like a war to me at least. To her it must have felt like hell, and I was definitely the devil. But the fact is, I know I can't be the devil, otherwise I would have off-loaded her in Siberia, and bade her *"hasta la vista baby."*

The *Vostok* rolled into Beijing at 5:46 a.m. and it filled me with joy and dread in equal measures. Joy that the journey was over, and we had made it to our destination, and dread that I would now have to get Sofia some medical attention and try and get her in a condition in which she would be capable of flying back to Milan early this afternoon.

Leaving the station and staggering along with our luggage on a dark, cold, wet morning we felt as miserable as we could get. The next hour was so totally ridiculous that under any other circumstances, it would make a great comedy sketch, equal to anything Woody Allen could dream up.

No one in Beijing speaks English. No one. Not that speaking English should be mandatory for any country, but how they managed to hold the Olympics, God only knows. This is not a criticism, just a fact. And at that moment I really needed an English speaker.

We were waiting in a taxi rank. We didn't know where we were thinking to go next. As we shuffled to the front of the queue, I had the idea to reach a hospital. Sofia was really in a bad way, every symptom of a heavy virus, and worst of all for me, she was not making any sense whatsoever, so was incapable of telling me how ill she really was.

I started asking all the people in the queue if they spoke English and where was a hospital. To say the clock was ticking is an understatement. She had a flight to catch, and really had to be on it. I was headed to Shanghai. Finally, someone understood what we needed and when we reached the front of the queue, he jabbered away to the taxi driver. I was relieved, for about five minutes - the time it took for him to reach and drop us off outside what looked like a very closed building, presumably, a hospital.

I wandered around the building, looking for a door, and finally found an entrance, which could have been the staff access - it looked like the rear of the building. No joy, I was told it was closed and there were no foreign patients allowed inside. Although I noted that there was a department for nuclear research! Aren't hospitals open 24/7? Aren't they supposed to serve all those that are sick? Anyway, we were getting nowhere. I had a brainwave, the airport was new, there must be a medical centre.

When I say we were in the middle of nowhere, I am really *not* exaggerating. It was 6:30ish a.m. The hospital attempt had failed miserably. We stood with our bags like orphans on the street. Hansel and Gretel in a forest of buildings, lost. By some miracle, a taxi approached us. I jumped out into the middle of the street. It's fair to say, that by now I was in a state of panic. Sofia on the other hand was oblivious to all that was happening. Like the zombie I had been in Poland, she just tagged along behind the mad Englishman. A beautiful, yet sick, Italian zombie.

The clapped out, ancient taxi stopped, and I shouted, 'Airport!' at the driver. He must have loved me, his smile spread from ear-to-ear, he was going to make enough *yuan* to feed his family for a week.

Finally, reaching the airport, I felt an incredible sense of relief. The hospital idea had been one of madness, desperation and stupidity, all rolled together in a massive ball of panic. We sought out the medical centre, and I finally I was able to hand Sofia over to someone who knew what they were doing. And they spoke English.

I waited outside for the verdict, fretting that they would say she was unable to travel. After half an hour I was called in and told Sofia may have a gallbladder or stomach infection. They gave us details of a hospital she should be taken to. If it was a stomach infection, I wanted to get back on the *Vostok* and set light to the dining car. The doctor would not give an opinion on whether Sofia could travel. Her blood pressure was normal, I nearly asked them to check mine, and she had no temperature. We left the medical team filled with uncertainty.

She looked ill, and I wasn't convinced she should fly today. I was desperate for her, and the condition she was in. This was supposed to be an amazing journey of a lifetime across Russia, fulfilling one of our traveling ambitions. It had descended into the *Holiday from Hell*. We were in our own reality TV show.

Other than some paracetamol there was not much the medical team could do other than wish us good luck. But luck was something I had been out of since leaving London.

We had time before she was due to fly. I dragged her to a café, and we forlornly sat considering our options. Sofia was adamant she would catch her flight. I have no idea why, but I agreed on one condition. She had to drink and eat something. I force fed her tea and a sandwich, which she resisted, but the look on my face and threat of taking her to another hospital, made her reluctantly comply. After the meal she started to feel a little better. Decision made; she was returning to Milan.

I called one of her friends and explained the situation, and she promised to collect her at the airport and get her to a doctor. There was not much more I could do, other than hope for the best. I waved her goodbye with a heavy heart, my fingers crossed, and a massive feeling of relief. Was I being selfish? Yes, but I had so far rolled from one panic situation to another, and in fairness it was beginning to take a toll on me. I nearly called it a day and jumped on the flight with her. This was the second time I had considered cutting and running. But something in me, some quiet determination, told me to keep going. Told me the difficult days were behind me, and that things would come good.

We look back at the time we spent on the Trans-Siberian as an adventure that took a bad turn. Yes, it could have gone better, but it could also have got worse. Yet nothing will take away the majesty of what we saw, and the experiences we lived through in those seven days. The bleak wildness of the Russian Steppe will live in my memory for ever. We have often spoken of those days, and normally we end up laughing at the madness of it all. Sometimes the bad days prove to be the ones we recall with the fondest memory. We travelled again, Sofia and I, and the next time it was to Nepal, and this time it was me that got sick. And I can honestly say, she was much more caring and understanding than I had been on the *Vostok*.

It wasn't even midday, but this day already felt like a

week. Shanghai was calling and I planned to reach there by the evening. Courtesy of a high-speed train that the Japanese would be proud of, and the English could only dream about, I reached my next destination early in the evening and checked into my hotel. I was exhausted, stressed, tired, hungry and most of all dirty. I had not taken a shower for nine days. The day had been yet another nightmare. I worried for Sofia, who would now be flying over Russia. I hadn't slept in a bed since Berlin, so the enormous one I now stared at was so inviting. But first there were some hygiene requirements to take care of, and a stomach to fill.

Later that evening, I was wide awake. A surge of adrenaline had washed through me after eating and to exhaust myself, I took a stroll to the Shanghai Bund, a mile-long promenade that runs along the waterfront of the Huangpu River. Later, on returning to the hotel, which had a magnificent view down to the old city, a city within a city, I finally gave in to exhaustion, and crashed out.

Day 12 Shanghai

In which a new *old* city is discovered for the first time, and the recent troubled past is left there, in the past

"The rise or fall of Shanghai means the birth or death of the whole nation." - Chiang Kai Shek

Shanghai… just the name conjures thoughts of the exotic and ancient empires. But this is the heart of a modern empire, and the *Red Dragon* goes from strength to strength.

The previous night's visit to The Bund had given me a taste of just how far China has come in such a short time. Mao's communism has given way to raging commercialism. The smell of money was almost as heavy as the smell of fumes from the ever-crowded roads. The Bund had been shrouded in mist, so that evening I was determined to visit again to get a clear shot of the skyline on *the other side.*

Mo Du really is a *Magic City.* The first impression impresses on a grand scale, and that never diminishes. It's one big, lively, frenetic city. With a blend of old and new, I see it as a cross between Hong Kong and Bangkok. The energy oozes from every building and street. Very quickly I understand I will never be able to see all there is to see. In the few days available to me I'll be running at pace, and that's like everyone else here. Running to keep up with everyone else.

Steven Spielberg clearly knew what Shanghai had to offer, with his 1980s movies, *Empire of The Sun* and *Indiana Jones and The Temple of Doom.* Those movies had left me in the Shanghai of the past, and I was not fully ready for the Shanghai of today. Big, modern and brash, an equal to any American metropolis. But here I was venturing out filled with expectation and an open mind.

From my hotel window I looked down onto the red tiled roofs of what looked like a shanty town. The old quarter, now surrounded by giant skyscrapers, was my first destination. It sat like a cornered animal under attack from a wolf pack. Shanghai is a city you could walk, if you had the legs for it. And after almost motionless days on the Trans-Siberian Railway, I really was ready to stretch my legs, and seek out all that I could.

From the cold and snow of Siberia, I now found myself in a land of rain and mist. A city of umbrellas presented itself - they were everywhere.

Wandering around the narrow streets, with the smells of steaming food, and red lanterns everywhere, I was transported back to a bygone age. I ventured into the Yuyang Bazaar and gardens. Hidden away were Buddhist temples and quaint little shops. Numerous restaurants abound, and after my starvation on the train, I was anxious to tuck into some genuine Chinese cuisine. I was not disappointed. The dim sum was amazing, and nearly as tasty as the crab, which was exceptional, and all so ridiculously cheap.

Tucked away, I stumbled upon a kind of department store. It was filled with small outlets and stalls selling everything under the sun, from tourist goods to clothes and food. I didn't see many *gweilo*, but with so many gift stores, I assumed that many of those around me were Chinese tourists. That evening I asked the hotel staff, and they said the biggest tourist groups were Chinese, people with money to spend, and anxious to visit their own country and get spending.

The buildings looked old and gave me the feeling that I was really in the beating heart of the city. Yes, the skyscrapers were impressive, but here was Old Shanghai, the one I was looking for. My hope being that the wolves would be kept at bay, and that the area was protected from development.

How often had I travelled and seen the result of *progress* on a place? Too often; and was there any progress? Perhaps it's best to call it evolution. We hanker for the old and enjoy the new. Take London or New York - cities constantly evolving. I'm sure people would not look at those two great cities and be-cry the evolution. And the new great cities like Shanghai would evolve and hopefully be mindful of its roots. If one day I were to return, I would still hope to be able to walk these crowded little streets and buy some trinkets and crab.

I walked and walked, sometimes aimlessly, not really knowing or caring where I was. I figured if I got really lost, grabbing a taxi would be easy enough to reach my hotel. I felt so relaxed and at ease. The pace of the city was frenetic, but my pace had been numbed by my journey thus far. I just moved from one street to another, absorbing all I saw. Eventually, I ended up at Shanghai's equivalent of Oxford Street or 5th Avenue. Nanjing Road is a brash, designer shop-fronted, endless stretch of opulence and wealth. As dusk set, I saw groups of 100 to 200 mainly middle and old aged women gathering for synchronised dancing. It wasn't really dancing, and it wasn't Tai Chi, I'm not sure what it was, but music blared out. I stood and watched in fascination. The idea of such a gathering and expression in the centre of Regent Street in London was too unbelievable. But this was happening and not in one location - on my stroll down the Nanjing Road, I stumbled across a number of these groups. It looked like fun. I nearly joined in, but out of a misplaced embarrassment held back and just stared. The fervent shoppers were clearly too busy spending all those newly acquired yuan, or had seen the show too many times, and they scurried past, totally ignoring what was going on.

How different are we, people? Maybe this, let's call it street dancing, had been going on for years. In the morning I had seen Tai Chi groups, but that had been in parks and along the river front. This was happening in the middle of a busy shopping street. The bright lights of the shops reflected in the shiny floor tiles, and music gave a party atmosphere. Shopping here took on a whole new feel. I didn't hang around to see how long the event lasted, but I witnessed a good hour of it.

Centred around the Maoming Road I found the former French quarter, which was totally lacking in French people. Why is it there are no British or German quarters anywhere? Many times, on my travels I have run into French quarters. It seems they leave their mark, even if they are few in numbers. It was a refreshing break from the high-rises, with quirky smaller buildings housing French coffee shops and speciality clothes and art outlets. I felt as I was in another city altogether. Totally charming, and a welcome contrast, with no glaring lights and signs. Another kind of city within a city. The French enclave, and earlier the *old city* enclave. Shanghai was throwing up surprise after surprise.

Mao Zedong lived here, and his former house is today converted into a museum. The small building is another contrast to the skyscrapers and looked just like some workers' cottages I had seen in Copenhagen. He'd turn in his grave if he could see the impact of the west on China, all that money sloshing around. China is only second to the U.S. in number of billionaires, and they are catching up fast!

Finally, I found my way back to The Bund, hoping

for the elusive skyline photo. The place was packed with what must be assumed to be Chinese tourists. I was stopped a few times and asked if I would speak with people. They wanted to practice their English. This was very different from what I had witnessed some years earlier in Tiananmen Square in Beijing, when I was repeatedly stopped to have my photo taken with people. That was in my Sting look-alike days. My new Phil Collins look was either not so popular, or they had seen enough *gweilo* to no longer be surprised by our presence.

These were the new rich with eight percent GDP figures, whilst we back in England struggled with austerity. The smart money was now yuan.

And boy did they know how to spend it. Fancy German cars crawled the busy streets, and Gucci handbags were everywhere. And I'm not talking about the $20 knockoffs you see being sold on street corners in the West, these were the real McCoy.

My first full day had been exhausting, exhilarating, and left me wanting more. I was looking forward to tomorrow. With aching feet and a full stomach, I collapsed into the best sleep I'd experienced since leaving London.

Day 13 Shanghai Kamikaze

In which the city keeps throwing up new surprises

"New York may be the city that never sleeps, but Shanghai doesn't even sit down, and not just because there is no room." - Patricia Marx.

The tall buildings surrounded me, I thought I was in New York. Skyscrapers abound in Shanghai. On my second day in this ever-fascinating city I had crossed to the *other side*. A ferry took me across the Huangpu River. It felt like the business district of any large city on a Sunday morning - quiet and sterile. Now up close, I marvelled at the incredible structures I had tried to photograph from The Bund the previous evenings. These giants now towered over me.

The Oriental Pearl Tower was not the tallest, but probably the most impressive. It looked like an architect after too much Baijiu had played around with a chopstick and decided to squeeze it through two onions. It looked all wrong, but seemed to work, and certainly put on a colourful show at night.

I didn't hang around too long. The gleaming modern buildings were not really my thing. I had been enticed the previous day, and was looking for something a bit more authentic and earthy. I came back, crossed to the other side of the river, but this time through The Bund Sightseeing Tunnel, a small train car ride through the tunnel that passes under the Huangpu River. A sound and light extravaganza.

I was getting the exercise I craved trying to walk this city. The sights and sounds hit me fast and furious. Crossing any road, you took your life in your hands. In most cities the green walking man sign means it's safe to cross. In Shanghai, the man is clearly running and not walking - and for good reason. If you walk, you may not make it to the other side. The cars, and especially motor bikes, drive straight through, irrespective of the traffic signal colour. I thought Phnom Penh in Cambodia was bad, but at least there, the vehicles stopped rather than hit you. In Shanghai I was *winged* by a scooter - many of them are electric so you don't hear them coming at you. I shouted after the *Kamikaze*, but he sped off.

I made it to the former Duolun Road, aptly renamed Cultural Road, a really charming district of traditional buildings. The area was an equal to the French Quarter, with tea rooms and antiques. My day was fast passing, and I was on a whistle-stop tour, so I moved on. I took the metro to the *art* district of Tiazifang, a pedestrian warren of small streets selling arts and crafts. More tea rooms and shops selling unusual clothes that looked like they had come straight out of a design collage. There were bars and cafes that were trying to be anything but Chinese.

I walked. And walked more. I found what I was really after, the *In* place. Xintiandi, an area of restored traditional houses, cafes, restaurants and bars. I was moving with the *In* crowd and I didn't even know it! I settled into a bar to be told this good news by a sweet local barmaid. I liked the place, even if it was somewhat predictable - it made a pleasant change from all I had seen.

What disturbed me with this city that offered so much was that it was clear there was so much more to come. There were numerous construction sites, scaffolding and cranes reaching for the skies. The Chinese GDP didn't look like it was going to slow down any day soon. Come back in a few years and there would be a forest full of new tower blocks. I'm not sure if this thought made me happy or sad. Looking back now, whilst I had thoroughly enjoyed my stay in Shanghai, and achieved another ambition on my travel list, I didn't feel a compunction to return. Not like I do with Hong Kong, or New York, or Paris, and let's not speak of my hometown, because London really is one of the greatest cities of the world.

After more wonderful Chinese cuisine, I started the long walk back to my hotel. But still Shanghai held a treat for me. It was pitch dark as I passed a park off the shopping drag. I heard music spilling out of the gates into the night and ventured in to find the source. To my amazement, the spectacle of around 80 waltzing couples. Was I in Vienna? I stood and watched. I was transported back to Buenos Aires where I had seen tango on streets throughout the city, and Catania on Sicily where, on warm summer evenings, they gather to dance around a fountain in the main piazza. The joy on people faces... It costs nothing to dance, you don't need a Rolex or Mercedes, just find a partner, or dance on your own. Fred and Ginger would be smiling down on Shanghai at that moment at such a sight. Surely one of the best examples of bringing what we do best in the west to the east!

They were dancing in the streets of Shanghai, and probably all over the world. It makes you think about what are the important things in life - often the most simple and least expensive. Money can buy so much, but there is so much money cannot buy - perhaps the most important things: joy, friends, love. Those dancers made a weary tourist feel very happy, and like those I have seen before expressing the most basic of joys, I will remember them always.

Day 14 Shanghai to Shenzhen

When sharing a train ride with a family makes Phil think of home

"Even if you're on the right track, you'll get run over if you stay there." - Will Rogers

My time in China was coming to an end. Hong Kong and the Pacific Ocean were calling me. Shanghai had eased and refreshed my mind. At the start of my stay, I was exhausted from what had passed before; the trip across Siberia, Sofia's illness and my general unease that I may be on the wrong track. I had chosen trains and ships to emulate Phileas and thus far I had been derailed mentally, although thankfully not literally. I was still on schedule to reach my next milestone, the Pacific Ocean.

With a few hours to kill, I ventured back to the Yuyuan Bazaar. It was a colourful, thriving place selling all the usual suspects: shark fins, lanterns and ying yang balls. I bought a few small Christmas decorations to add to my bulging luggage. I bought those things for the sake of it and not because I needed them. Consumerism, spend, spend, spend, and for no good reason.

The Chinese spit a lot. Quite why beats me. I had been told a story that a few years back, but not too many, the internal Chinese flights had spittoons in the aisles. Now that is something I wouldn't want to see. They spit on the floor, in bins and rarely in a handkerchief. The bird flu in the early part of the century must have loved this national affliction.

I found the people rather detached. They are probably getting used to us *gweilo* being around - like we are now seeing them pop up all over the place. The world is getting smaller, as the saying goes, but trying to go around it still makes it feel like a pretty big place to me.

The Shanghai South Train Station is a very impressive place. A gigantic modern spaceship of a structure. No less impressive from inside as it is out. I enjoyed sitting around watching the people preparing for their journeys, buying noodles and snacks, many with enormous bags and luggage. Clearly there were some long trips being made and that included mine. I bought a ticket for the overnight ride south to Shenzhen - just across the border was Hong Kong, and my ship to the Americas. Now, being an old hand of such train journeys, I also loaded up with noodles and chocolate. Although the samovars were not as impressive as those on the Trans-Siberian, they still did the job, and were in constant demand.

I was in a four-bunk compartment with a Chinese family of three, mum, dad and a very young baby. Foreigners were in short supply on my train. There was me, and me. The smart people were flying, but as this wasn't an option for me, I hit the rails. Buses had been considered, but were much slower and, I'm sure, less comfortable. In some countries trains are not really an option. South America for example, where I had travelled mainly on buses. Later I would think about all these train journeys and put value to the pace of life and the people I could meet. I hadn't slept with a baby in the room for twenty plus years when my two were newly born, so this journey was throwing up unexpected surprises.

Hour after hour we rolled through China. I imagined endless countryside and farms, but not so. There's a revolution going on in communist China, and it's got a name - capitalism. Yes, there were a few farms, but mostly it was factories and endless electricity pylons. Like Russia, the railways were responsible for evolving society around them with new towns and cities popping up. An anomaly is that under many of the pylons are small market gardens - patches of green in the otherwise grey landscape. I tried to put a logic to it but failed.

Trains are an important part of Chinese life and featured in *Last Train Home*, a Chinese documentary that highlights the annual migration of people to their homelands for the Chinese New Year. The largest movement of people on the planet. More than 130 million people shifting to and from their home villages and towns. Fortunately, I was missing the crush as this normally takes place in spring.

China was advancing at pace, and we were all being carried along by it, and increasingly dependent on it. If the Sleeping Giant caught a cold, we would all be sneezing and coughing to another stock market crash. But surely the economic pace would have to slow at some point? How many pairs of sneakers or television sets did anyone really need?

I wanted to see some green, but all I saw was grey. In Russia it had been white. I would have to wait for another long train journey, the one across Meiguo, The Beautiful Country, as the Chinese call the United States of America, before I would see yellow and green in abundance. Until then it would be the grey of China and then the Pacific blue.

Seeing my travelling family and the care and love those new parents were showing their little girl got to me a little. It made me think of home, and my kids and family. I was a million miles from home, and still had a long way to go.

I left my new family to the compartment and wandered up and down the train for some hours, eating my noodles and drinking tea, taking in as much as I could. The train was full and people were gathered in groups, laughing and joking, dozing and eating. The train had it all, a whole society seemingly enjoying the arduous journey south, determined to make the most of what may have felt like a holiday to some.

Exhausted and no longer able to keep my eyes open, I sneaked into the tiny compartment like a bull in a China shop, wearily climbed up to my bunk and settled in for the night.

Day 15 Shenzhen to Hong Kong

Where Phileas and Phil cross paths for the one and only time

"I see that it is by no means useless to travel, if a man wants to see something new." - Passepartout

I spent the night on a top bunk in our four-bunk sleeper carriage. The baby girl was just a few weeks old. She was a cute little thing, wrapped in a quilted pink jumpsuit. It was still cold outside, although the train's heating worked a treat. That's one of the joys of travel, you never know who you will meet.

We couldn't speak much to each other, there were a few hand signals, nods and grunts, but I somehow managed to explain I have two children. They let me hold that little baby for a while, whilst they took photos. I guess I was the first foreigner Pinky would meet. Who knows? Maybe I would be the only one!

They were a nice family, loving and caring and sweet. The world is full of people who are exactly the same. A similar train ride in Vietnam came flashing back to me. Shared food, photos and smiles.

The carriage was a step up from the one on my fateful attempt to reach Moscow. There was even a jug of water and small posy of flowers. Nice touch.

The train had travelled through a dark Chinese night. I think it stopped a couple of times, but our carriage was a full house, so no one came in and woke me. Occasionally I would hear Pinky cry, but I soon drifted back off. The motion of a train was proving a powerful sleeping draught. Breakfast was pot noodles and jasmine tea, finished just in time as we approached the border city of Shenzhen at 9 a.m. across from Hong Kong. It had been a 1,000-mile trip from Shanghai, passing through four provinces. What I saw was a lot of grey, like most of China appeared to me. City after city rolled by - their names I never heard before. I had crossed another vast country; two down, one to go.

In London I had applied for a new passport, and upon receiving it, immediately sorted out visas for the U.S.A., Russia and China. The only three visas I would need. The three superpowers all in my shiny new passport before any stamps found their way in. The hardest to get should have been the easiest, the U.S.A. I shouldn't have even needed one. Whenever I previously visited the States, I completed the green waiver form on arrival. For some reason, arriving by sea meant you required a visa. So off I trundled to the U.S. Embassy in London. The queue was around the block. Curiously, no mobile phones were allowed inside. A few days later I realised the Chinese and Russians didn't have the same paranoia. But to enter the U.S. Embassy, anyone carrying a phone who wanted to go in had to leave it with someone or somewhere.

An entrepreneurial pharmacy around the corner was doing a roaring trade. When I finally got inside it was mayhem. Eventually, reaching a counter to speak with someone, I was told I didn't need a visa to enter the U.S.A., being British. I explained that I was arriving on a cargo ship. That had raised a few eyebrows. I explained my mission, *should I choose to accept it*, to emulate Phileas Fogg. I'm not sure the agent believed me - he asked me who Phileas Fogg was. Fortunately, he called another agent. Luckily, this one had read the book, and could see the poetry of my need. I'm now the proud owner of a ten-year U.S.A. entry visa. Bingo.

It is worth noting that my first entry stamp in my new passport was cancelled way back in Belarus, before I reached the big three. That seemed a lifetime ago.

Disembarking the train from Shanghai, I wasn't really sure where I should go. I was headed for the border. Fortunately, I ran into a guy called David, who got off my train and seemed like a veteran of the route. He navigated me through immigration. I was one of many crossing that border - it seemed like the whole of China was trying to cross to the former land of fish-n-chips and afternoon tea. Once through immigration, there was a train to Kowloon Tung.

I was back in Hong Kong. It was the only city where Phileas Fogg and I were to cross paths on our routes around the world; both heading off from here to the *New World*. In a former life I had visited so many times that it felt like home… the smells and hustle and bustle. Over 30 years it hadn't changed too much, but maybe I was wrong, maybe it felt different, or at least to me. Yes of course there were more skyscrapers, but the vibe… was it really the same? Everything and nothing changes.

From Shanghai I had booked a hotel room, which turned out to be a real dive. I opted for a part of town I didn't know, close to the Prince Edward metro. It was the smallest room I had ever stayed in - putting up strong competition to one I had the misfortune to use in Tokyo. I planned to stay just the one night. I showered and hit the tourist trail.

For the record, I have a love affair with Hong Kong, having previously visited on many occasions. It's easy to navigate this small, crowded, vibrant city. Christopher Nolan had seen what Hong Kong had to offer and shot a *Batman* movie here. From Chicago to Hong Kong, the caped crusader certainly got around.

I was headed to The Peak, the hill overlooking the city on Hong Kong Island. I made my way down to the *Star Ferry* to cross over from Kowloon. Nothing here had changed. Same ferries with their reversible benches, cheap as peanuts. Same tram up the hill.

Memories of previous visits and experiences flooded back to me, as they do now. So many wonderful times. Life really was a joy. My wife and I had visited here, in difficult times, and that really saddened me to think we had not fully experienced this city at a time of happiness. Later visits with my kids and lovers had been more joyous. Places, like music and food, can evoke the deepest and most profound of memories. Whenever I see a plastic stool, I think of sitting in the fish market near the Temple Road, eating seafood with my children. I love the fact that I can be transported in this way to a place or person.

I had once spent three weeks here working, which had been frenetic. The city had one gear, fifth. Those three weeks had slaughtered me, mentally and physically. One had to marvel at the tenacity of people to function and thrive at this pace. But that trip had afforded me some down time, and the good and bad fortune to have a car to drive. I explored every corner of the island and Kowloon side, and I had not been disappointed. From Aberdeen to Happy Valley, and Stanley to Sha Tin, my eyes opened wide to all I was to see. A snake shop in a Wan Chai backstreet and haute cuisine at The Peak. Everything was here; you only had to look for it. And even better if you could get off the beaten track and find what others didn't. This was my speciality, looking for something different, something new. Like finding a gem only I would see, and I would treasure.

I loved my day as a tourist back in what felt like my own backyard. I breathed in the moment and the memories. A little R and R after the journey since leaving London. Memories on every street corner. I looked forward to the few days I would spend stepping back in time.

What lodges in our brains and never leaves? Incidents, sights, smells, people. That day presented me with one. One I would never forget, just like that minibus in Belarus was now imbedded in me. I had stumbled across the fish market in Wan Chai. And there in the middle of the street was a giant fish. It must have been a metre square, with an enormous head disproportionate to its body. Its poor mouth sucking in the air - sucking in its last breaths. Its fate clearly already decided. I mean that fish knew time was up, otherwise what was it doing in the middle of a street? I was mesmerised. I couldn't look away, try as I may, from the horrible sight of it. It got worse; that poor fish had to suffer for the show, the spectacle to follow. Slowly, a small crowd gathered as the shop owner worked himself into a lather. He was hollering at the top of his voice to get people's attention. Only he knew what was to come. With a massive cleaver and in two rapid swipes he severed that giant head from its body. He then separated them, pushed them apart, head and body. And what stayed with me, that minibus of a memory, is that fish's mouth still gasping for breath, no longer attached to its body. Instantly I was transported to the jungles of Vietnam, Colonel Kurtz getting what was due to him, as a water buffalo is slaughtered outside, in *Apocalypse Now*. Fish and buffalo facing their same fate, with indifference and dignity.

That night I went to the Philippe Starck designed Felix Restaurant and bar at The View atop the Peninsula Hotel in Tsim Sha Tsui. We had celebrated my daughter's 21st birthday there. The view is spectacular across to *the island*, the best in town. I realise I am not the first to reference this amazing restaurant - Jean-Dominique Bauby mentioned it in *The Diving Bell and the Butterfly*, as he dictates his amazing true story through the blinking of his left eyelid.

Nostalgia hangs heavy in the Fragrant Harbour. We've all seen the TV shows, movies and news reels. Suzie Wong, junks and drunks. The ancient trolleys and modern skyscrapers. And let me say, so it's on the record, I miss the old airport, Kai Tak Airport. The airplanes would make their final approach over Kowloon so low that you felt you could pluck clothing off a washing line. And hurtling down the runway for take-off, the plane would lift off just before reaching the drink - some didn't make it. The new airport at Lantau just doesn't have the same thrill.

And yet amid all the mayhem, escape is possible. I recall a ferry trip out to Chen Chau, a small island about an hour's ride from the city. The ferry was packed with weekenders looking to leave the cut and thrust and money making behind for a while. You can buy fish and seafood from the fishermen at the local market on arrival and take it still kicking and screaming to a quayside restaurant to cook in whatever manner you prefer, and all for a few dollars. Add an ice-cold Tsingtao beer, and the chaos of city life soon evaporates.

James Bond showed up here a few times, notably most recently in *Skyfall* - assassinations, and casinos - what a life. The casinos are in Macau, an ever shorter, as the boats get faster, 60-mile ferry ride from Kowloon. Anyone who has ever entered the casinos of Macau will surely realise Las Vegas is for fun; Macau is where the real money spins out of control. One place I went to was seven stories of casino floors. And every one of them packed to the rafters. The atmosphere was electric, jostling and shoving to get to a table, to place a bet. It wasn't fun, it was panic driven addiction. I mean, how much money did people have to lose? It seems quite a lot! They say Vegas was built on *losers*, what built Macau? Even bigger losers? It's certainly not so flashy, and it sure isn't as much fun as the Entertainment Capital of the World. But along with so many sights in and around Hong Kong, it's definitely something to not be missed.

It had been a day to remember, a day to reflect and a day to embrace what would come. From a bunk on a train in China to a swanky restaurant in Hong Kong. I never left this city without vowing to return. And I cannot say that about many cities. London, obviously, but I have been lucky enough to live there - New York, Paris. The great cities just get better with age.

Travel Tip: if visiting The View, go to the restrooms, they are the most spectacular urinal view I have ever witnessed!

Day 16 Hong Kong Island

In which living in the present reminds Phil of living in the past

"You can leave Hong Kong, but it will never leave you." - Nury Vittachi

In some cities I feel like a tourist, but my familiarity with Hong Kong left me feeling like I was home, or near to it. Over the years I had spent a great deal of time here. It gets under the skin. I always leave knowing I'll return.

In two days, I would set sail for the New World, and leave Asia behind. I was excited at the prospect, and just a little apprehensive. But most of all I was curious, not of what I would find in America, but about the ocean crossing. I had never attempted anything like it before. The new holds a smidgen of fear - the familiar, we can cope with. I'm not a sailor. I bought a canoe once and sold it a week later. I've never owned a boat. I wouldn't know what rope to pull. The sea is my friend, but to swim and dive in. Being a certified diver, I love the sea and all it holds, and I have little fear of it. But sailing across such vast oceans was another thing altogether. Sailing is not totally accurate, the vessels that would carry me on the Pacific and later Atlantic were enormous container ships. There would be no rope pulling - but there would also be no gin and tonics or romanticism.

For now, I was on my old stomping ground and intended to cram in as much as possible. The Trans-Siberian and rigours of reaching China were behind me. Things hadn't gone according to plan exactly, but I arrived in the former colony on time, and ready to kick back a little before climbing aboard.

Hong Kong is small, but there is so much to see that any visitor with only a few days is spoilt for choice. Over the years as a tourist and on business I had seen a lot, so I approached these few days with nostalgia, and set out to revisit some on my favourite places.

We think of Hong Kong as a city, but it is much more. It's larger than people realise - over 1,000 square kilometres. Small compared to almost anywhere - over 100 times smaller than New York State for example. But small is good, it's easy to navigate. The public transportation is extensive and cheap. So, finding your way around is easy and quick and consequently I was going to be able to squeeze a lot into a couple of days.

I was staying in a hotel in Kowloon which placed me on more familiar territory; Tsim Sha Tsui was closer to the action, the harbour and passage to the islands. I had found a decent hotel and after settling in, hit the streets in search of my old haunts.

Tsim Sha Tsui is the most vibrant district on the Kowloon side: shops and restaurants everywhere and for some reason a predominance of electrical shops selling the latest gadgets. Most are run by people of Indian descent for some reason, as are the tailors, knocking out made to measure suits in a couple of days. Hong Kong always was, and despite the *handover* in 1997, always will be, a trading hub and melting pot of different peoples.

The politics of the place have brought a change in atmosphere that is tangible. The British rule of 156 years of was being washed away, but left a few stains, and the Red Dragon now running the place was breathing its very special brand of fire. The surface looked unchanged, albeit for the regular new skyscraper arrivals, but under the shiny surface, the loss of freedom was stirring the masses.

Before crossing to Hong Kong Island for my bus to

Stanley Village, I wandered the waterfront. Looking across at the giants opposite, I could have been back on The Bund. The skyline was changing quicker than the Italian, Arturo Brachetti, the quick-change artist I had once seen, who could change outfits 80 times in a single show. I was sure I would never look across and see the same sight - tomorrow would be different.

A yellow film of pollution clung to the surface of the harbour as the Star Ferry plied its trade, and boats of all shapes and sizes spilt their exhausts onto the water. I photographed a young boy pulling a kung fu stance in front of a Bruce Lee statue on the promenade. Lee was a legend in Hong Kong, revered for his movies. The man, who died so young at 32, opened all our eyes to martial arts, and kung fu in particular. Carl Douglas sang it best, *"Everybody was kung fu fighting."*

Photo opportunities abounded and I hadn't reached the ferry yet. The sights were subject enough, but the people took centre stage, well at least for me. A group of yellow capped and panted school kids were gathered under a bridge, drawing what they saw across the water. They had seen it a hundred times, so perhaps it was all in a day's schooling. For us visitors it was a spectacle. Those kids had better be quick, another giant could be built in the next few minutes and the scene would change, like the passing of the gathering clouds.

A short walk had me on a *Star Ferry* across to Hong Kong Island. I would never get bored of making the crossing. The old-style ferries chugging across one of the busiest harbours in the world. Shiny skyscrapers were being erected all around, but the old ferry was the most impressive sight of the day. Any tourist would readily pay 20 times the paltry asking price for the privilege of making this crossing.

The Chinese have this lazy looking approach to most

they do, as if everything is effortless. Of course, it's not so, but the effect given is almost nonchalant. They make casting-off ropes and berthing look as simple as lighting a cigarette.

For all its brashness, there are hidden gems to be found everywhere. A bus ride to Stanley takes you through some rare green spaces before arriving on the south side of the island. Suddenly the hustle and bustle are left behind to be replaced by a charming village atmosphere. Venturing further, you can reach Shek-O village, with fantastic seafood restaurants, a stone's throw from the beach. Stanley has always been a tourist destination, and its market sells all that any tourist could devour from lucky heads with four faces to oriental lanterns. I like the place not so much for the market, but for the restaurants and waterfront. Relaxed cafes playing jazz drop the tempo down a few notches. On previous extended visits to Hong Kong, I would amble over to Stanley on a Sunday and shake the city out of my system for a few hours. To get even more laid back, I would take the ferry over to Lamma Island for the day and sometimes overnight.

From Stanley I took buses along the south side towards Aberdeen, passing the million-dollar apartments at Repulse Bay towering over the beach, offering those with the money a beach residence and escape from the day to day stresses of money making in Central. I could have been in any wealthy district in the world with a beach front: the Caribbean, Australia's Gold Coast. They all looked much the same, perhaps even had the same people living in those swanky palaces.

I'm not knocking it, the place was nice enough, if somewhat forced. We all deserve time to kick back and de-stress. And if ever there were a group that needed it, the Hong Kongers would be near the top of the list. Just walking around the business districts exhausted me. I had stayed a couple of weeks once, manning an office and charging around the place. I lost four kilos during that stay. The frenetic energy was burning the calories quicker than I could replace them with crispy duck and dim sum.

That evening I returned to Hong Kong Island and Aberdeen. It had grown up since my last visit, but the Jumbo restaurant was still there, along with other floating monster eateries. Whatever we may think about such places as being for tourists, make no mistake, they are nearly always full of locals, and we are surely all eating the same food. Seldom will anyone eat a meal and be disappointed. Ancient looking junks still plied their trade and gave the place a feeling of authenticity. Bruce Lee was here in the 70s classic *Enter the Dragon*, and perhaps more up to date, and certainly with negative connotations, the Jumbo restaurant featured in *Contagion* - the less we say about that, the better.

Hong Kong has been a movie directors' friend for many years. Every corner offers something different. James Bond has come to love the place, with so many visits during his spying career!

Day 17 Hong Kong Kowloon side

Where a return to a quiet island, that now proves to be anything like its old self

"Crisis or not, nothing should interfere with tea!" - David Niven as Phileas Fogg

There are many restaurants offering afternoon tea to be found around the world, and a few are exceptional: The Ritz and Savoy in London, The Plaza in New York. Add to the list The Peninsula in Hong Kong. I was tucking into a clotted cream and jam covered scone and sipping Darjeeling tea and feeling like one of the millionaires from Repulse Bay.

The day had started with sticky buns and jasmine tea at a small cafe in a back street off the Nathan Road. I was fully enjoying a culinary explosion, to knock my Trans-Siberian eating experience into the long grass. Hong Kong had it all, and I was working through the very long list.

The cafe was buzzing - it was probably buzzing every day, seven days a week, 52 weeks a year. There is peace to be found quietly sitting in a little cafe, minding my own business. Watching the movement in front of my eyes, as if looking into a fish tank. Outside, a storm of people rushing around, is raging. While inside I felt relaxed and calm, knowing I shall soon enter the maelstrom. As I stretched out my tea, I thought about the many visits I had made to the city.

Back in the early 1990s on a Sunday afternoon, I had taken a ferry out to Lantau Island with a local colleague, Paul. His birth name was Chinese, but like many Asians he gave himself a western name in his teens; a friend of Paul's had decided to call himself Ringo! Where were the other two? We were going to visit the giant Buddha at the Po Lin Monastery. It was a lazy ferry ride to what was an almost deserted island. Taking a bus up to the monastery, we passed through rolling green hills, finally arriving and marvelling at the spectacle in front of us.

The Tian Tan Buddha statue is enormous at 34 metres high. I wonder if the people who decided to build it knew what Lantau was to become. Perhaps if they had, they would have had second thoughts. We climbed the steps up to the foot of the Buddha - the view was fantastic. Was this really Hong Kong? Peace, tranquillity, green. Later, walking some of the trails, we stopped and looked down at a smaller island. Lying just off Lantau, was Chek Lap Kok. Paul told me that they were to remove the top of the island and put it in the sea, to build the new Hong Kong International Airport. I looked in disbelief and did not know whether to take him seriously or not.

A few years later, those industrious Hong Kongers had performed a miracle, and the new airport, one of the largest in the world, was opened in 1998. They had indeed lopped the top off Chek Lap Kok and chucked it into the sea! Where I had looked down onto green hills with a green island beyond, it is now not only an airport but a city. Some 200 inhabitants had farmed that island in the 1950s, now the airport serves over 200 destinations globally and handles over 70 million passengers a year. That's what they call progress! I hope those farmers were well compensated for moving out.

That airport island was named after a fish, because of its shape, and because the perch (I had tried to eat perch on the Trans-Siberian) frequented the waters around the island. I've passed through many times, and there's nothing fishy about the place now, other than the sushi on sale in the airport terminal.

You can still take a ferry to Lantau, but I resisted. I never returned to the monastery, but the Tian Tan Buddha is truly lodged in my memory. A sunny summer day, with clear blue skies highlighting the majesty of that Buddha sitting proudly on its plateau, surveying all it saw. You can see that Buddha, far in the distance, from the high-speed train that carries you to the airport. I like to think it's not smiling, but at least at peace.

I finally dragged myself out into the storm of people and wandered around. Walking as much as my legs would permit, because I was heading out to sea soon, and I didn't imagine there would be much chance to stretch my legs on the Pacific. I was very wrong on that count!

I thought about the movie *"The Painted Veil"* as I strolled the backstreets, seeing red lanterns fluttering in the breeze. Ed Norton in China, doing his bit to combat cholera and partaking of opium. The English were selling opium in the times of Phileas and making a killing; annually £1.3 billion equivalent today. Puffing on a pipe now will see you convicted and given a stretch, but back in those days it was as common as a pint of beer. Passepartout hung out in one of those Hong Kong opium dens, and the experience resulted in him getting split up from his master, Phileas, and costing Mr Fogg a fair packet. Hong Kong must have been one hell of a place back in the *good old days*.

I contacted the port agent, who confirmed the *MV Hanjin Athens* was on schedule, and that I could join the following day any time after 10 a.m. It's fair to say I had a heightened expectation. I had never really been to sea, and yet I was now to embark on a voyage comparatively few had taken. The manner in which I was travelling would cut that number down much further. Cargo ship over cruise liner!

I kept walking, and as I walked, I was on the lookout for somewhere selling scented oils. I had been told that lavender oil behind my ears would prevent seasickness. Eventually, with the oil purchased, I headed for afternoon tea, and a little luxury before braving the waves.

My days in Hong Kong only reminded me of what I already knew; Honkers is one amazing place. It's right up there with the best and equal to all. Even with the changes that the *handover* brought, the city has tried, and in the main succeeded, to hold on to its identity. I didn't hope I would return; I knew I would.

Day 18 Hong Kong *MV Hanjin Athens*

In which Phil discovers the extent to which the coming weeks may prove a challenge

"As for Phileas Fogg, it seemed just as if the typhoon were a part of his programme." - Jules Verne

No more dim sum for me, I was blowing out of Hong Kong today on fair winds across the Pacific. Well, that's what I thought as I had breakfast in a French cafe, tucked away close to my hotel. Honkers would always hold a place in my heart. So many visits and experiences in this city that never seemed to sleep. Waking up in New York is great, but this was the real city that didn't sleep! Frenetic energy bounced off the skyscrapers, through the back alleys and engulfed all those who lived there. It always felt as if it was about the money, and perhaps it was, but I think it was something else, something in the psychology of the people, something generic, impatience.

I had previously tried to leave Hong Kong. Twice nature had played its part, summoning typhoons of biblical proportions to trap me in that frantic city. Huge hoardings had taken to the skies with rage. Building swayed, and the tempest kept all the junks in their safe harbours. On one occasion I was held captive for three days; me and two plane loads of Taiwanese tourists, quickly evaporating the hotel's supply of provisions.

But the fair skies held no one captive this day, and it was time for me to leave. Destiny on the world's great oceans was awaiting me. The *MV Hanjin Athens* was to carry me to the *new world*.

I took the MTR and then a taxi to the port, registered my passport, collected a port pass and walked to the ship. She was another form of skyscraper, towering above the quay at least five containers higher than the deck level - a modern-day *Titanic*. At 279 metres, she was ten metres longer than that ill-fated liner. There would be no icebergs on the Pacific to jeopardise our crossing. But some weeks later, the *Titanic* would announce itself to me, on the bridge of another vessel, as we sailed north of her fateful encounter with nature. No icebergs on that voyage, global warming had taken care of such obstacles, so far south from the polar bears and Eskimos.

Most of Phileas Fogg's travel was by steamship. The *SS Mongolia* took him from Brindisi, Italy to Bombay, India, and was 2,800 tons. The *Hanjin Athens* weighed in at 67,000 tons. And towering above me, she looked every kilo of it.

Climbing the companionway to the ship's deck, the size impressed upon me. Finally, puffing for breath, I arrived on the deck to be greeted by the second officer, Norman, a friendly sort, who took and introduced me to a much sterner sort, Captain Schmidt. All the officers were German bar one, Vlad who was Croatian; all the remaining crew were Filipinos. So, seven Germans, one Croat, 17 Filipinos, and one Brit, that made 26 of us, heading off into the calming seas of the Pacific. No women on board. I thought about this a little, why? Was it the same on all commercial vessels plying the world's oceans? And seldom did I see officers and crew mix. Clearly, they knew their place, unlike me, who was oblivious to such protocols. And I can tell you, eating spicy food with the Filipinos made a welcome respite from the meat and potatoes I regularly ate in the officers' dining room. Thankfully, I only gave up eating meat a couple of years later, otherwise I would have been in serious trouble.

There would only be two stops before heading to Los Angeles. Both were in China, in places I had never heard of: Ningbo and Yangshan, and at neither was anyone allowed to leave the ship. So, climbing up to the deck would be the last I would feel the earth beneath my feet until we reached The City of Lights.

The captain was a pleasant enough man, but not one to regale us with sea-faring yarns over bottles of Johnnie Walker. If in advance of meeting him I had been asked to describe a German sea captain, I would have won top prize. Tallish, fattish, moustachioed, stern and most of all with no sense of humour whatsoever. As would be proven one fateful night after a few too many bottles of wine had been consumed.

But to balance that lasting impression of him, I would have to add competent, thorough, reliable and if any pirates were to try and take this ship, I would want him at the helm over Tom Hanks as Captain Phillips. I like Tom, but Captain Schmidt would have just looked at those approaching speed boats and they would have turned tail and sped away. He never offered his first name, the captain; and neither did I. He always referred to me as Mr Hill. Probably that German thing they do with *du* and *sie*.

He really showed his true colours at my first dining experience. I was to eat with the officers, so I entered the officers' mess and went to sit down at one of the tables. The captain looked up, twitched his moustache and said, 'No Mr Hill, you have your own table,' and pointed to a table with one chair. I felt like a schoolboy given a dunce's hat and told to stand in the corner. My initial thoughts had been confirmed. It's fair to say we never quite clicked. Although this was not true of my relationship with the other officers. I later discovered the captain had only recently taken over command of the

95

Hanjin Athens, so perhaps he was stamping his authority in front of his men. Or maybe he just didn't like the idea of paying guests, even if I was the only one. I mean this wasn't a cruise liner, there were no cabaret shows and afternoon bingo. However, I later discovered there was a swimming pool, which turned out to be the size of a jacuzzi and never had any water in it.

Norman showed me to my cabin, and I must admit I was pleasantly surprised. Spacious enough to have a double bed and sofa. Carpeted, and that counts for something, as I was to learn, crossing the Atlantic. There was a TV with a DVD player, which was to prove a life saver. In the officers' lounge there was a supply of books and DVDs, so I would never be short of entertainment. But no TV signal, no streaming services. No Wi-Fi or phone connections. I would be sailing blind and adrift, and mostly on my own.

It had never dawned on me that there would be such little contact with other human beings. All on board had their role to play, and I was an inconsequence to it. What was I even doing there? They carried cargo not passengers. Cabins like mine were normally reserved for the ship's owners and their guests. Occasionally, a passage like mine was booked, but never in winter. No, I quickly realised I was alone, and whilst this was nothing new to me, the circumstances made it feel more intense. *"Here am I floating round my tin can"* far away from all I have known. And yet unlike Major Tom, there was something I could do. I cleared my mind and set out to fill my coming 17 days with a new routine.

To many people, 17 days may not seem like a long time, but being isolated in that *tin can* would certainly not be everyone's *cup of tea*. What is strange to me is that everything I did appeared so heightened to my senses and recollection. The books I read, or movies that I saw, so many come back to me in waves of memory, even if they were not particularly impressing at the time. I remember a book by Frederick Forsyth that ordinarily I may not have even read - but it stays with me. Something about the experience I subjected myself to left an imprint. Nutella… I cannot see a jar without being taken back to the mid-Pacific and my sneaking down to the galley every evening to steal a couple of spoonfuls from a massive jar that I found, but which was never available to the officers. Why not? Didn't officers like Nutella?

Containers were being loaded all day. The ship could carry more than 5000 TEU (twenty-foot equivalent units), and it looked like we would be quite full. The loading was made with clockwork precision. A truck would stop under the moveable crane and the container would be lifted and raised and swung over the deck to its resting place deep in the hold of the ship. As the loading progressed, the towers of containers grew higher, reaching 12 blocks in height. On average seven below deck and five above. The loading continued all evening and into the night.

I was anxious to get on our way, but big commerce took precedence over global travellers. Phileas would have bribed the captain to set off early. Mind you, if he tried that with Captain Schmidt, he wouldn't have much joy!

I stood on the platform at the side of the bridge and watched the loading, mesmerised by the synchronicity. But as I stood and took a final look at the glittering lights of the skyscrapers in the distance, a feeling of calm washed over me as I accepted my fate of the coming weeks, and the endless ocean ahead of me.

Day 19 Pacific Castaway

In which walking amongst giants becomes a daily routine

"WILSON!!!" - Tom Hanks as Chuck Noland

We cast off and I became a castaway. I would be alone most of the voyage to Los Angeles, but not really experience loneliness. The *Hanjin Athens* was my island in the Pacific, but unlike Tom, I was on the move, and heading home.

The sea can be a lonely place, that's for sure. Quite how single yachtsmen and women cope, God only knows. And add nature to the misery, and all it has to throw at you. My friend Magnus, the one who helped me out of the mess I got myself into in Belarus, is a sailor. He's crossed the Atlantic in a ship far smaller than the one I was taking for my return to Europe - he sure has some tales to tell.

I was concerned about seasickness more than loneliness. The literature I had received from the booking agent stressed the need to prepare. Of course, this was an oversight on my part. I assumed they would have some magic cure on-board. I was to find out there was no medical officer. Getting sick or having an accident was not a good idea. Fortunately, neither was to befall me. Nor seasickness.

At 1:35 a.m. the *Hanjin Athens* cast off from the quay in Hong Kong. Actually, we were pulled off by a tug. Either way, we were no longer connected to Asia and were on our way.

I had a nice feeling. A feeling that there was no turning back. My journey around the world was suddenly real. No ducking out now and heading home. By the time we reached Long Beach I would be more than halfway through my journey. Past the point of no return. The only way was east, and I had America and Europe in my sights. But there was still the little matter of crossing the world's largest ocean. Despite my circumstances and all that had gone before in reaching this point, I still felt a disconnect from what I was actually doing; I mean, in my attempt to emulate Phileas Fogg. I stood on the bridge and looked down at us leaving Hong Kong and I felt detached from the reality in which I found myself. I felt like a puppet, and someone was pulling my strings, and I was just bouncing along as directed. And here I am now on a boat. Whoopee!

This was no cruise; there was no spa or 24-hour buffet. There were no fellow passengers with which to hang out. There was me, myself, I - and a whole lot of ocean to cross.

I went to bed and slept surprisingly well for my first night at sea. My first breakfast and at my own special table - *"All By Myself, Don't Wanna Be, All…"* I bet if Celine had been on board she would be dining at the captain's table! Through gritted teeth I managed some eggs and toast. I reluctantly got used to the dining arrangements after a couple of days, accepting this was how life was at sea. But not so. Crossing the Atlantic, I joined the officers for every meal.

Prior to starting my journey, I had set myself some personal objectives, and this *cruise* offered me the opportunity to realise them. Weight 90 kilos to be reduced to 80. Lousy Greek to be improved well enough to at least hold a reasonable conversation - I live in Greece for four months each summer, so my failure to master the language was, frankly, embarrassing. Fitness, my one pack needed to be increased to at least a two.

After breakfast, I walked around the deck. On the

previous day, the captain had told me to wear a hard hat, but as I set out on my first 600 metre circuit, I saw no one else with one. On the next walk I ditched the hat. Perhaps it was only needed in port, whilst loading? Anyway no one ever mentioned my missing hat, which was a massive relief, as I would have sweated buckets wearing one. I was walking among giants. The containers, stacked six or seven high, towered over me. They were connected to each other with metal lashings, and twist-locks secured the bottom ones to the deck. I had seen photos of containers coming loose in storms and flying overboard. Did Robert Redford's yacht get hit by one in *All Is Lost*? For my first few walks I passed these tower blocks with a little trepidation. By the end of the voyage, I wasn't even seeing them.

The day passed slowly, ending in a very quiet dinner. Once the captain left, I grabbed hold of Norman, who told me a little of what lay ahead on the voyage. We would take a northerly route, stopping at Yantian and Ningbo to load containers, then continue north, skirting Japan, and on towards the Bering Sea before turning east towards the States. He cheered me up when he said I should keep a look out for whales on my deck circuits. No mention of my not wearing the hard hat.

Day 20 Pacific Routine

Whereby setting a daily routine life on board is made more tolerable

"The first day one watches to see whether a routine will emerge: it is a routine that makes home." - Graham Greene

I wake, eat, walk, study, exercise, eat, walk, read, exercise, eat, read, watch, sleep. And then tomorrow I'll do it all again. Have I established a routine? You bet your life I have.

But isn't life just one big routine, or many small ones?

Born, live, die.

Born, childhood, education, work, marriage, kids, grandkids, die, etc.

Dr Seuss had me *bang to rights* when he said *"You have brains in your head. You have feet in your shoes. You can steer yourself in any direction you choose."* I did have a brain in my head, even if it was a bit *mushy* at times, my feet were well and truly in my boots, my direction was making 600 metre circuits of a floating island.

My new routine was mostly confined to the four walls of my cabin, the officers' mess and deck. By day three I had settled into it, and its very existence now governed my life. There were aspects I was struggling with. Study. I have never, and I really mean *never*, been studious. School completely passed me by. Higher education was not an option because a. we never had the money, and b. I was not bright enough. God only knows how I got myself to a position in life where I could make this journey!

I blame, or should I say thank, Margaret Thatcher. For all the derision from so many ill-informed quarters and well-informed quarters, she gave us British hope, aspiration and pride. No more power cuts due to strikes, no more living in a council flat, no more being the basket case of Europe. Yes, the *Empire* was long gone, but my generation had been shown a path we could follow. The path of *hope*. Not the phoney *Cool Britannia* that came later with Tony Blair. Maggie, for all the wrong turns she took, put us on the straight and narrow.

So, my Greek studies were well and truly hitting a wall. I could barely remember the alphabet, and the clue is in the word, Alpha Beta… As a Greek friend once told me, 'You speak Greek, you just don't know it!' It would only take a week before I completely gave up and took to reading thrillers as a replacement to studies in my routine.

This was an aspect of my character I have never understood. With some things I can be so patient, with an interest and desire to learn. But with others, I just give up so easily. It's like I just can't be bothered, and I have no idea why. Learning Greek was a case in point, as were languages in general really. Perhaps it's a British thing. Let's be honest we are pretty lousy in that department.

The exercise and walking were easy. And this was because they allowed me to escape the cabin. In the case of exercise, I escaped to what was known as *the gym*. The gym had two broken pieces of weightlifting equipment, an empty and extremely small swimming pool, a sauna and exercise bike. The sauna fascinated me as I just didn't get why it was there. Most fascinating of all was that it worked. I tried it a few times, but the thrill was short-lived, it felt like another level of confinement. Solitary, as opposed to the gym, which was the exercise yard.

The exercise bike proved to be my friend and salvation for two hours a day. I should say I don't cycle. I gave up around the age of 16. But that rickety old exercise bike got used every day. For the first week I tried reciting the Greek alphabet as I pedalled and stared out of the window at the passing Pacific.

Three days into this journey and the Pacific was beginning to calm me. I accepted my fate, just like I did, sitting in that cramped hot train carriage in Poland. Was I a fatalist? Had I always been one? I didn't think so, but perhaps I was. I often accepted my fate, although sometimes not without a struggle if it was appropriate. In Poland I had accepted it, fate. And with the days stretching ahead of me until reaching Los Angeles, I accepted it. I fixed my course, and my routine was the star that would bring me to my journey's end, my destination, my destiny!

There was a dayroom for the officers to use. Considering there were only eight of them, the room was extremely large. It was a place for them to hang out and socialise with each other. I rarely ever found anyone there, irrespective of the time of day. A large selection of videos could be found, along with books and a few board games. One of which was backgammon, a game I really enjoy playing. My father was born and brought up in Cairo, Egypt, by a Greek mother and English father. I think it was inevitable he would grow up playing backgammon. He also spoke five languages. Backgammon was the only thing he passed on to his four children. The languages would have been more useful, but he never found time to pass on such knowledge to us. Yes, he was around some of the time, but he apparently worked a lot. Later we would learn that he spent most of his free time at the *bookies*, betting on horses. Those *three-legged* horses were responsible for many aspects of my childhood.

That evening I ran into Frank, the lanky mid-20

something officer cadet. He wanted to know how to play backgammon, so I made it my mission to teach him on the evenings he was free. They would prove to not be too many. And after the *drinking night* that would follow, even fewer.

Day 21 Pacific Movies

In which a passion for movies is spoilt for choice, and a necessary distraction

"It rolls the mid-most waters of the world, the Indian Ocean and Atlantic being just its arms." - Herman Melville

Awake and adrift. It's 8 a.m. and sleeping is proving easier than I expected, with peaceful seas and a comfy bed.

The *Hanjin Athens* started this voyage in Italy, so I calculated that if I had joined her there, and then completed my journey as planned, it would have taken a total of 77 days. My new calculation put my travel at 65/66 days, so taking the trains to Hong Kong proved to be a good decision. And I was now an *anorak* with my newfound love of train travel. Phileas never had the Trans-Siberian option so took ships from Italy to India, and then after crossing India onward by ships to America.

In the late 1800s, there were quite a few steamships plying the shipping lanes, unlike today, when giants like the *Hanjin Athens* can carry enormous volumes of cargo. Many of those old ships would carry passengers, also unlike today when very few do. Vlad told me that it was pretty rare to have any of the three cabins occupied. There were times when I could believe I was on a ghost ship. I can wander through the ship and deck for hours and see no one. There are five movies named *Ghost Ship*, so it's clearly a popular theme. And how many more from disaster to war movies feature the sea, and Pacific in particular? *Captain Phillips* stands out as a more recent container ship movie, but before that was a Danish film, *A Hijacking*. Those pesky Somalians dashing around and causing so much trouble.

I rifled through the ship's video collection, hoping to find something nautical, but alas, no such luck. I was regularly raiding that collection looking for some evening entertainment. There were the usual classics, such as *The Godfather*, *A Few Good Men*, and *Platoon*; I had seen them all before, and would surely see them all again. Actually, there were hundreds of movies. Some I had never heard of, so I set about working my way through some of the more obscure, and there were quite a few Bs and Cs among them. But a few stood out for a future second watch. *Enchanted April* and *Inside Man*, both such different movies, and both left their impact on me. *Enchanted April* really is soppy but perhaps in my isolated state, a little gentle romance was exactly what I needed. It left me feeling melancholy. And the Annette Bening and Warren Beatty remake of *Love Affair* has become one of my most watched movies. Poor Warren waiting at the top of the *Empire State Building*, I wonder how many times he has been stood up in this life! Even if Annette had very good reason for not making the date. But *all's well that ends well*, and those *star-struck lovers*, got together in the end, and in real life!

I was spoilt for choice and even if many of those movies were real dross, I had more than enough decent ones to see me through the voyage. And I was very thankful for that, I can tell you.

My exercise routine, of 3-4 hours per day, is beginning to show results, with loosening clothing. I may even have to make another hole in my belt. My first day on board, I struggled to make ten press-ups in a session, now I'm hitting 30. It may not sound a lot, but I was happy enough. Eventually I would reach 50 and do those three times a day. With two more weeks still to go, was I finally going to make a weight breakthrough?

That afternoon we ran into a wall of fog, and noticeably, the ship slowed. Norman, the second officer, told me we would be arriving late in Ningbo, our final stop. We would be prohibited from entering the port until the fog lifted. The fog made the *Hanjin Athens* feel even more like a ghost ship! We just seemed to be swallowed up by it. Spooky. Suddenly, I was on the *Mary Celeste*. I went up to the bridge and looked at some of the navigation. Thank heavens for radar! The view from the bridge didn't instil much confidence, as I could barely see the prow of the ship. Ningbo was waiting for us somewhere out there. I was silently praying it wouldn't be like this crossing to the U.S.

Over dinner, I tried to engage more with the officers, however they really were very quiet. The captain's presence always seemed to have an effect on them. The crew, on the other hand, who I sometimes met on my walks, were much more open for a chat. I was invited to join them for dinner, which I did a couple of times and experienced the best food on the journey - Asian cuisine, hot and spicy - and I could sit with the Filipinos and chat with them.

Day 22 Pacific Ningbo

In which having no means of communicating can become addictive

"I realise now that there's a lot to be said for travelling if you want to see something new." - Passepartout

I was given a *Change of Time* sheet. Just like that, we fast-forwarded, and I lost four hours. My routine would be buggered!

My regime was the only thing to realise time against. And eating was by far the greatest influencer. Strict timing for each meal: 8:30 a.m., 12:30 p.m., and 6:30 p.m., never any change, even if the clocks did. With the loss of four hours, breakfast came very close to last night's dinner.

Most of the time I was craving some interesting food. Only the Filipinos offered me any relief from meat and two veg! We were in a ship, on the sea, and fish never appeared on the menu. That didn't add up for me.

Last night at 11 p.m. we finally berthed at Ningbo. Ningbo, I had never heard of it before, but it was a city of eight million Chinese. An anonymous city with a population close to London's. Not that we had any chance of catching a glimpse of it, either last night or today. The fog was lifting, but a mist persisted, and I couldn't even see the perimeter of the port. Ningbo was therefore nothing more than container cranes and a few vessels to me. A misty nothingness. We hung around in that nothingness until 2 p.m. No shore leave here, I guessed we were not there long enough, or perhaps being China we would need a visa. Whatever the situation, no one left the ship. Containers were loaded, the ship was really filling up. The towers of containers were reaching into the sky. My deck walks among the giants would prove more impressive and claustrophobic at the same time.

Tugs pulled us off the Ningbo quay, and we were no longer attached to China. The next time we would touch land it would be Long Beach, California. No mist or fog awaited us, only sun-filled skies. It would be 13 days before we arrived in the *New World*, 14 days when we added the extra one for crossing the dateline. Two weeks of isolation, two weeks that I saw as a personal challenge to my reserves of self-determination, strength and patience. And these two weeks would take me mentally to places I did not expect. I stood outside the bridge and waved farewell to Ningbo and China. I waved farewell to land and gave myself over to the sea.

No internet or communications meant no distractions. I'm a news follower as a rule, so what was happening in the world was lost to me. I remember being in Greece once and only discovering that Osama bin Laden had been found and killed two weeks after it happened. How had I missed that little trinket? I was adrift and had so little of my world available to me. No shops, bars, restaurants, friends, family. Nothing. Just me and the occasional shipmate, and a great big ship slowly slipping through the calm waters of the Pacific.

The mealtimes were becoming something of a challenge in themselves. I was getting hacked-off with feeling like a naughty schoolboy, expelled to eat on my own. I tried to engage with the officers but shouting across the room was tiresome and downright daft. I decided to give thought as to how I could get some communication going. The officer's dayroom could present opportunities, and if it did, I would seize them!

Day 23 Pacific Safety Drill

In which we learn how to survive in the case of emergency

"My destination is no longer a place, rather a new way of seeing." - Marcel Proust

There were two large lifeboats, one either side of the ship - port and starboard (I'm sure there were others), and not many of us. I had read a few books about castaways and shipwrecks and a history of survival at sea under extreme conditions. Looking at these luxury lifeboats, we would not be resorting to drinking seawater or cannibalism. And we were following international shipping lanes, so safety had not been a consideration or worry for me. As with most situations I find myself in in life, I just assume everything will turn out alright.

And it was alright. There were no dramas on my voyage across the Pacific. No fires or pirate attacks. No sickness outbreaks and no severe storms. Plain sailing all the way.

Any dramas I encountered were all in my head, and in fairness, there were not too many of them.

Norman explained during the safety drill that the sea was a *6* today and would be climbing to an *8* as we approached Japan. My sailing had mostly been restricted to Greek ferries, and you could definitely feel a *6*. But on a mammoth, such as the *Hanjin Athens*, it felt like a mild swell.

The safety drill involved gathering near the lifeboats, in our life vests, in the case of an emergency and understanding what to do. To this day I'm not sure what I should have done other than get in one. There was probably a standard operating procedure to follow, but nothing sunk in for me. So, I just stood around watching the others, most of whom looked as bored as I was feeling.

Books were filling my day. The dayroom offered a wide selection, many in German. However, there were enough English language books to go around the world with! I chose some authors I wouldn't normally read. A Chris Cleave book about a refugee, *The Other Hand*, made me think a lot on a subject which I knew so little about. And one thing it made me think about was so many refugees in search of a promised land, taking to the seas in flimsy crafts barely able to stay afloat. What incredible risks people were prepared to take to escape from the lives they knew, venturing into the unknown.

Another book, a totally different type of fiction, but one that returns to me frequently, and for all the wrong reasons, is Frederick Forsyth's *The Afghan*. It's not the main plot that I think about, I lost that over the years, something about a cargo ship carrying arms, or a bomb. No, it's the scenes early in the book of random, small (if death can be a small thing!), attacks. A terrorist stabbing a random passer-by to death. Since reading that book, I have been reminded of so many of these attacks happening; cars ploughing into pedestrians, stabbings… and what disturbs me; I don't remember such attacks before reading the book. It leaves me asking, what came first, the attacks or the book?

How often are the scenarios of a book or movie played out in real life? For instance, the movie *Contagion*, need I say more?

I was shown a room with washing and cleaning facilities, a blessing, my clothing was beginning to look a real mess. With washing machines and dryers readily available, I washed everything I carried with me. The rest of the afternoon was spent on the bridge and Vlad explained how the ship could be run by a single person. Similar to a plane, the course is pre-set, running on autopilot. Quite an array of panels with switches, buttons and screens left a momentary impression of a mad scientist in a *Bond* movie, just waiting to launch an unexpected attack on a super-power.

To my surprise, I found a few people in the officer's dayroom after dinner, and we had a couple of drinks. They were quite relaxed and opened up about some of their shipmates. I'll keep most of what was said to myself, but it's fair to say there was a fair amount of *bitching* going on. The ship was not as harmonious as I had imagined, and there were clearly some issues between the German and Filipino officers. 'What Filipino officers?' I asked. I hadn't seen any. Three of them existed; I had probably taken them for crew, they certainly didn't dine in the officer's mess.

It was a pleasant change from my evenings so far, watching videos and sleeping early. I hoped it would be frequently repeated; I was to be disappointed. No more than twice I week did I ever find someone *out for the evening*.

A massive plus was meeting Thomas the Chief Engineer. He invited me for a tour of his engine room the day after tomorrow. And more importantly he pointed me to a stash of more recent DVDs. A technology jump from the videos, and some entertaining additions to my *movies to be watched* list.

Day 24 Pacific Bering Sea

In which Phil reflects on life and his father

"Fix your course on a star and you'll navigate any storm." - Leonardo da Vinci

There is no point looking at a map between two points and assuming you'll take the direct route. I learned that from flying - look at any trans-continental route map and there will be a curve in it. Our giant globe teaches us that. So, we were heading north to the Bering Sea, even though we should be heading east. As the day unfolds, we pass some small Japanese islands and keep going north.

Time and days are fusing into one. The sea and sky seldom change; mostly clear, mostly calm. With each day I become more thoughtful, more reflective, more connected to myself, my life. So much has changed for me in recent years, there is a lot to think on. Changed for me, or by me? Most people I have met in life kind of *trip* through it. Change has come about not as a conscious thought or decision, but by default. I guess I'm no different, however I can consider three or four major cross-roads where I made the change. As Barack Obama famously said, *"We are the change we have been waiting for."* I tried to be my change. The change I was waiting for!

I followed in my father's footsteps in one regard. He gambled. A habit, or perhaps a way of life he acquired when moving and living for the first time in England. This was after a life lived on the African continent. The move to England happened a few months before mine and my brother's birth, and that's a story also... My father would gamble on anything: horses, dogs, bingo, two flies walking across a tabletop. Pretty much anything you could gamble on. My gambling was with life. The gee-gees were his favourite flutter. He's 97 and still places his bets each day. Those gee-gees have probably kept him alive so long.

Some investments I made were high risk. My Gambling. They felt like three-legged nags sometimes. No risk, no gain. I had come from very little, so there was only one way to go!

The most important and recent change was to stop working (as I had known it) and try and live life doing what I wanted to. This had happened in 2006 after some intense working years, and at the time of a relationship break-up with someone I dearly loved. I recognise now that whilst that decision changed everything for me, there had been one adverse effect: I had become closed. I built walls around myself so high that not only could someone not reach me, but I was trapped and could not reach out to anyone.

That time in my life also coincided with my decision to buy a small house on a Greek island. I still live on that little island, splitting my time between there and England, and with some travels thrown in. Travels like this one! I can't complain; I love my life. I wouldn't swap it with anyone I know. That big change, the 2006 one, I have never looked back on with any remorse or regret. I made my bed, and I was well and truly lying in it!

This time afloat gave me time to think. And think I did, and about so much. My past, well, that I could not change, but this journey made me think of the future, and what I may need to change. I spent a great deal of time thinking of what I wanted to do. I had already decided to leave London. As great a city as it was, I needed to move on. I would head west, and a few years later, further west. I currently live in Devon.

But my thoughts also drifted to relationships. Family, friends and inevitably loved ones. Here I was on stony ground. I know I could and should have done better in my life. As I roamed the ship and marched around the deck, I consciously decided to *try harder*. But trying harder is not as easy as it sounds. If I'm honest I could only give myself a 6 out of 10 since completing my journey around the world. So, yes, I must keep *trying even harder*.

We didn't enter the Bering Sea, but we got close. We skirted south of it, and slowly but surely started to turn east. East again. London Calling; but London was still a long way off. It felt like I was making good progress, but the reality was that I was still less than halfway through my journey.

Day 25 Pacific Engine Room

In which it is discovered that this journey around the world could be completed more quickly, but for a decision to save money, and burn less fuel

"He who travels in the Barque of Peter had better not look too closely into the engine room." - Ronald Knox

Massive engines grinding away carrying us forward to America. There to off-load their precious cargoes, mostly Chinese, before about-turning and churning their way back to Europe.

Thomas was as good as his word, and over breakfast arranged for me to tour his *pride and joy:* the engine room.

It was cavernous, and having seen where the containers were stored, I had difficulty understanding where the space was to fit everything now stretching out before me. A giant 10-cylinder monster was burning 80 litres of oil (HFO, heavy fuel oil, cheaper than most others) per minute. And that was on slow running, and we were running slow. On fast running of 24 plus knots, which the ship was easily capable of, the giant would burn 140 litres per minute. The cost saving had us running slow, around 19 knots.

Didn't they realise I was in a race against time? They were adding days to my journey! Phileas would definitely have been dipping into his travel-bag, pulling a few thousand pounds out to bribe Thomas with, and insisting on *"More speed"*.

Despite wearing ear protectors, the place was deafening, and I was struggling to understand anything Thomas was telling me. From what I could see, he had three crew working with him. They appeared to spend all their time checking things, mostly dials, panels and screens. There was an incredible array of such things in addition to the mechanical equipment. What I had seen on the bridge looked totally insignificant compared to the engine room. I was reminded of the scene at the nuclear reactor in *The China Syndrome*, or perhaps a more recent comparison would be the TV series *Chernobyl*. Thomas explained some of the functions, but it was all gobbledygook to me, he could have been speaking Korean. I diligently nodded my understanding. How often do we do that in life? Nod along to something that is totally incomprehensible.

The place was spotless, so perhaps that's what took up most of the time, cleaning every drop of oil and dirt away with rags. And now I can wonder what went wrong a year later when a fire broke out in one of the cargo holds. And what panic would have ensued here in the engine room and throughout the ship? There were 200 containers flooded with extinguisher water, and their cargoes lost. And at what cost? The ship had to stop for inspection and off-loading. Lost days cost money in the cargo business. Lost days would cost something for me - time - so I was thankful of no such dramas during my voyage on the *Hanjin Athens*.

I saw my first sea-life today as I walked the deck. A pod of six or seven dolphins were racing the ship, and they were winning. No slow running from them! They were a beautiful, majestic sight.

In the afternoon I spent an hour on the bridge. I never felt welcome there, but with so few options to explore, I took my chances there from time to time. We were treated to one of the most spectacular sunsets I have ever witnessed. Storm clouds in a heavy sky hung over us, but far on the horizon there was the front edge of those clouds, and a thick line of sun was setting. The sun was an enormous white ball with yellows and oranges stretching either side of it. I couldn't work out why we were even seeing this sunset. The sun sets in the west, I thought we were heading east. I was confused but too embarrassed to ask the captain to explain. What was important was that I was seeing this amazing sight before my eyes. A spectacle that would never be bettered. Or so I thought!

Day 26 Pacific Ocean

In which thinking about the life of a sailor makes Phil convinced it's not the life for him

"Any damn fool can navigate the world sober. It takes a really good sailor to do it drunk." - Sir Francis Chichester

It was more than a week since I'd had any contact with the outside world. No emails, phone calls, messages - nothing of the global communication we have become accustomed to. I thought I would miss the connection, but strangely I realised I didn't. I am old enough to remember life before the technological revolution, when I would have to go to a phone box to call a girlfriend, and hope she was in. I mean, where would she have been? We didn't have a lot of choices in those days: the local cinema or a greasy spoon cafe. Now it would be a text message to arrange a date at a Cineplex, followed by McDonalds. That assumes that youngsters actually meet each other these days - perhaps they just have WhatsApp dates.

So, what if I disappeared from the social media world? Who was going to miss me for a couple of months? I'm single with grown up kids, and most people I knew were accustomed to my going AWOL. In fact, not many people I knew were even aware I was on this trip, let alone this ship! I have been accused of being secretive, and maybe I am, it's just that I didn't broadcast what I was doing. No blog to follow or social media posts. The only person following me was me and I still hadn't fully worked out how I was going from one place to another. Drifting, but drifting east. Actually, I had been drifting for some years now.

When I first contemplated the life of a sailor, I had

thought, 'How boring,' but maybe it was only a question of time and adjustment. Speaking with my shipmates, the officers and crew, not one of them voiced a desire for any other career choice. They loved life on the ocean waves. I was eight days into this voyage, and I could not really see the appeal. Months away from home and loved ones, living a very solitary existence. But they seemed to revel in it, and the money wasn't bad either. Maybe being away from those you love made you love them even more - made you appreciate them. Something for me to consider.

When we left Hong Kong, I really had no idea what to expect, but I was open to the possibility of peacefulness - after all, we were sailing the Pacific. And peaceful it was, often churning away on the exercise bike in the gym; looking out at the unending ocean, I would almost fall into a trance. Hours would pass without my noticing.

And slowly but surely this peacefulness swept over me. I found my routine of reading, exercising, walking, eating and sleeping was coming naturally now. Days blurred into each other, and I blended into my environment and seemed to come to be as one with it. Sometimes I felt as if I was not really there, just a shadow or ghost of me was, as if the crew couldn't see me. Like I was part of the furniture or a passing wave. I consciously noticed myself relaxing, and this state evolved as the journey continued. There was something happening to me, and I let it happen.

I had cause to think about the waves, and me being one. It reminded me of a *Reconnection* therapy I explored a couple of years earlier. There had been a point in this no physical contact experience when I became a wave. Literally. That's the best way I can recall and describe it. My body felt like it was the sea; not in the sea, but part of it. As if I was in an *out of body* state. And perhaps that was where I was now. A wave in this vast ocean, rolling towards a point, a time, when I would crash onto a shore, and be released back onto terra firma and life as I had known it. Like emerging from that therapy session back into the light of day, back onto solid ground. The same, but subtly different.

The tranquillity was shattered that evening, in the officers' lounge that until now, had always been empty. I found some cards and poker chips. Around 8 p.m. I was joined by First Officer Mark and an officer cadet, Frank. Nice guys both, but normally very quiet. We hung out for a while and beer and wine appeared. We played some poker, and more booze kept miraculously appearing. A flood gate opened, and no one knew how, or had the inclination, to close it. It was a release from the peace, from the ocean, to let loose a little.

I should say that I had never seen anyone drink more than one beer onboard. The myth of drunken sailors had been dispelled for me; this lot were almost teetotallers. But not that night. And after that night I never saw them drink again. And I obeyed the clear message of the captain when, the next morning, he appeared at my cabin for the one and only time and said in a very serious and commanding German way, 'Mr Hill, please do not get my officers drunk again,' and he wasn't smiling as he said it. He turned to leave, shaking his head, and I swear I heard him mutter, 'Passengers,' as he marched away. I mean, they were grown men, their alcohol intake had nothing to do with me!

On the subject of myths, I want to dispel another - *A girl in every port.* Life had moved on since Jack Nicholson in *The Last Detail,* or Gene Kelly in *Anchors Aweigh.* There was even a movie called *A Girl in Every Port* - trust Groucho Marx to get right on the money. Where all these ports and girls were, was yet to be discovered. In my naive fantasy, before setting sail, I had imagined some *interesting* nights ashore with drunken sailors. I recalled the life I had seen in Pattaya, Thailand many years before when four U.S. Navy boats off-loaded their horny sailors into that quiet little town - well it was a little town in those days. Banners were strung across the main street *"Welcome U.S. Navy"*, and there were muscle-laden MPs patrolling the streets - and what a welcome they received. Those navy boys would always remember Pattaya. It really was straight out of a movie. There were no banners for the *Hanjin Athens*. In fact, there were hardly any ports. Seafaring was certainly not the fun it used to be!

After that night, which in fairness, I don't recall with much clearness or clarity, life returned to normal. Quiet and peaceful, and the poker night was not mentioned again. A brief, perhaps necessary, interlude to stir the waters of this calming ocean, with only the occasional black look from the captain to remind me that it ever happened.

Day 27 Pacific Headache

In which the day after the night before was best forgotten about; however, the captain didn't see things that way

"His headache was still sitting over his right eye as if it had been nailed there." - Ian Fleming, *Moonraker*

My head was throbbing, and two doses of two paracetamol were having little impact. I hadn't drunk alcohol for some time, so the impact of the red wine and beer mix of the previous evening was having its effect on me.

In a dazed and confused state, something was nagging at me. Something I should remember this morning. Church. There was a Sunday morning service every week. I roused myself and made it just in time. Most of the officers and some of the crew were already gathered. It struck me as the only time I had seen them united, other than for the fire and safety drills. There was very little religion going on, with most of the time spent with my shipmates regaling seafaring tales. Some involved accidents at sea, some dubious port calls. It was nice to see them a little relaxed. The captain invited everyone to have a drink, just the one. As I opted for water, I would swear he gave me a *look*.

It was after the church service and just before lunch that he showed up at my cabin. His message was loud and clear. I had been a naughty boy once, and once was enough. I mean it was only a few drinks, and I was no Captain Jack Sparrow, and we were certainly not *Pirates of the Caribbean!* Anyway, I got the captain's message... and vowed to myself to behave for my last week on board.

My head was still spinning. I sluggishly went outside, hoping the pure air would sober me up. It had worked for Passepartout after his drunken night in Hong Kong. Alas I didn't get the same reaction. However, lunch helped, but not much. I spent most of the afternoon watching movies during which I dropped off for regular catnaps. Thankfully, the sea was being kind and with no major swells I would come through the experience relatively unscathed. The only lasting effect was the increased distance between me and the captain. I didn't really speak with him much after this day. But as I was leaving, *checking out,* in Long Beach, he clearly cheered up as we chatted about my experience on his ship. He was probably just pleased to see the back of me.

Dinner was a quiet affair, so I imagined word may have got around about the previous evening. No one paid me much attention, but then, that was not totally new to me. I took it in my stride but was relieved the following morning when there were a few more smiles and some friendly words. Just maybe, some of those other officers had wished they could have joined in the fun!

I mean to say, come on guys, we drank a bit too much. By the standards of some of my evenings on my little Greek island home, this had been a walk in the park. Some of those ouzo-fuelled nights would be memorable, if only I could remember them!

Day 28 Pacific Across the Date Line

Where one day becomes two and the journey feels like it is being stretched that little bit longer

"There are two days in the year that we cannot do anything, yesterday and tomorrow." - Mahatma Gandhi

Today was a day like no other on this entire trip, I would live it twice. Not quite *Groundhog Day*, with Bill Murray suffering the fate of the same day repeatedly, but strange all the same. Today we would cross the Date Line.

I had been heading east, towards the sun, and with each degree of longitude I lost four minutes. Phileas was a clever chap, but he missed this vital piece of information. It's hard to believe, isn't it?

It took Phileas 52 days to reach the 180 meridian, which left him 28 to complete his race against time and win his bet. I had got here in 28 days and would definitely take longer on the second leg back to London. I planned stops along the way, whereas Phileas dashed across the United States to catch his vessel to Liverpool.

Living in London, I often visited beautiful Greenwich and stood over the Prime Meridian Line. Now, here I was, halfway around the world, sailing over its opposite number. This journey was sure throwing up situations I would never forget.

I had crossed the Date Line a few times in my life, but always by plane. It felt weird enough then, losing or gaining a day. Now by ship, it was even stranger. I was gaining a day, which frankly I could do without. Psychologically it made my journey seem longer. In reality of course, the *Hanjin Athens* was going to take as long as she needed. Phileas, not accounting for the gain of a day, had nearly lost his bet.

125

The Date Line doesn't cross any land but does split some Eskimo inhabited islands in the Bering Sea. I crossed it without knowing, striding around the ship on my regular 600 metre circuits, desperate to shed a few kilos. Perhaps a diet of raw fish would help with that, although I've never seen any photos of skinny Eskimos; probably all that seal blubber they eat to survive the harsh climate they inhabit.

As with the Trans-Siberian, I was passing through multiple time-zones on this Pacific crossing. Fortunately, the ship kept up to date with them, so my body clock was functioning normally. I was now 12 hours ahead of Greenwich, and another 12 behind. The significance of my position also hit me. I had reached the milestone of being at the halfway point of my journey around the world. From here on in, I would be heading not only east, but also home.

Home, the very thought was almost abstract. Where was home? I had long forgotten about it. Days were lived full of movement. Home was static. I am reminded of a road trip across the U.S. On reaching our destination of Miami, I was relaxing with my son, and he asked, 'So where are we headed tomorrow?' But we weren't headed anywhere, we had arrived. No more endless roads, motels and diners. We were quite depressed. Being on the go, in movement, had been exhilarating. Road-trips will do that to you. A couple of years earlier, I spent five months in a camper van going around Australia; never staying more than a day or so at one place. Moving on, and on. When finally arriving back at my starting point in Perth, I felt an enormous sense of loss. That journey had been completed, the circle closed, but there was no elation or joy, just an emptiness. I missed the roads, the unknown, the expectation and not knowing what was coming in the next hours or days.

There is certainly something to be said about roaming, the freedom of place and mind. I was now heading home, and when reaching it, how would I feel? I pushed such thoughts from my mind; there would be time enough for such reflection. And reflect I would because this trip, more than any I had previously made, was having, and would have, a lasting effect on me.

My normal routine was shattered by the fire alarm. The captain had decided to wake us all up from our peaceful Pacific slumber with a fire drill. And this really did feel like something straight out of *Captain Phillips*. I was in my cabin, so gathering my life saving essentials, and getting to the muster point, B Deck by the lifeboats, in good time gave me some brownie points with the skipper.

Suddenly, there were people everywhere. The most I was to see on the entire voyage. I was wearing warm clothes and had my emergency suit, which was bagged, and my life jacket. Ready to abandon ship and finding it all a welcome distraction from my daily regime, I was loving it.

The idea was to simulate a fire in the engine room. The captain looked to be in his element. Red hard hats and overalls everywhere. Apart from two crew in full fire-fighting shiny silver top to toe suits with special visored hoods. I was the only one without a lifesaving overall on. Officers first, crew second, passengers last. But I was having fun watching the two fire-fighting boys get their act together. They looked like spacemen - *"Ground control to Major Tom"*. We all trundled down to the engine room, and the fire-fighting heroes connected hoses and pretended to extinguish the fire. Actually, I think we all had fun that day, the only one not smiling was the captain. Thank God someone was taking this desperate situation seriously. Really, what would we do if there really was a fire? Fortunately, I was allowed to follow all the action eventually leading to an evacuation, simulated of course. We gathered around the lifeboats and acted out the scene to abandon ship. I was disappointed that we weren't required to get in the lifeboats - that would have been a blast. And then before we knew it, it was all over. We had survived the fire and were ready to continue the Pacific cruise.

I was to learn that 16 months after my voyage, a fire broke out on the *Hanjin Athens* south of the Suez Canal. My flippancy and humour at the drill was clearly misplaced. Fire at sea is certainly no laughing matter. The ship and crew survived, some of the cargo did not.

I missed the simulated pirate attack drill by a week. I'm sure that would have been even more fun. That evening, over a game of backgammon in the officers' lounge, which was a rarity, Frank told me some crew had to hide in secret chambers. I guess I was taking life on board to be very routine and straight forward, but the reality was that it was important work that had to be done well. A 270-metre ship with many millions of dollars of cargo isn't something to be taken lightly. They took things very seriously; they had their routine. I was just along for the ride, and thankfully I had my routine.

I lived this same day again. In fairness with my daily routine, it shouldn't be so much different from yesterday, which is today!

Except, it is different. The sea has changed from a flat calm to a fairly rough. The same day, calm and rough. Rough enough for us to feel it and me be told very firmly that I would not be walking any decks this morning. My daily routine was dismissed, and I was obliged to seek alternative ways to fill this unnecessary day.

The ship's rail is quite low, certainly no more than a metre high, and low enough for me initially to be a little spooked by it. Going overboard would be a one-way trip. I was limited to the gym, and my ever-faithful exercise bike.

During the afternoon, the wind dropped sufficiently to venture outside. I realised how much I missed the fresh air. I sucked it in. Little did I know the Atlantic would have me bound inside for almost the entire voyage. And it could drive you stir-crazy. I think what let me push on in a positive way was the fact that that voyage would be taking me ever closer to completing my journey. I would remain in good spirits throughout that internment. The winning line was in sight.

And as if to reward my patience, I was presented first with a rainbow to beat any I had seen, an enormous, coloured arch spanning the Pacific. Things are not done by halves out here in the middle of nature. The rainbow was followed by another pod of dolphins, and then a sunset so magnificent I just stood in awe at its majesty. Sailors will harp on about what they see at sea, and the sunsets regularly feature, and I was beginning to understand why. Nature is a beautiful thing, and the more remote you get from humanity the more spectacular it is. Leave the cities, noise, and light pollution behind, and see our world. Sunsets at sea and the stars in the desert. I was lucky enough to have once been out near Uluru in the middle of Australia, in the middle of nowhere, and the night sky took on a wonder I would never forget. Untold millions of twinkling stars filling vision beyond vision. And now I had the good fortune to be seeing this, the sun setting over the vastness of the Pacific Ocean. The sun a white golden orb surrounded by colours that no artist could paint. Oh, what a lucky man I am!

Day 29 Pacific Quiet

In which it's not always possible to keep one's chin up

"The end of all our exploring will be to arrive where we started." - T. S. Eliot

It goes that there is a peace before a storm. I didn't know I was heading into a storm, but by the following afternoon I was in the eye of it. Not a Pacific storm, but one within the depths of my mind.

My mood was low after the double-day yesterday. For sure, it was just psychological. I think the notion that I had one more day on the ship, one more day on the journey, one day more before returning home, had an impact on me. The truth was I wasn't in any hurry to return, but the feeling of being delayed did affect me. Nothing was waiting there for me that couldn't wait another day, week or month. I guess, I just wanted to *get on with it*!

Eventually, I would be sitting on a train, my final train, my train back to London and feeling so strange. Similar to today, but the reverse, a low mood because my journey was over, not because it was delayed.

Now, with my low mood, I considered what was coming next. How life would be after getting off this floating prison. Stepping back onto land, feeling the earth, solid ground, under my feet instead of the ocean waves. I planned to walk, and then walk some more.

But once something is in your head, it's hard to purge it. Like lying awake at night, the same stupid issue going around. Thoughts invading your sleeping time. Sometimes with me it's a song or something I've watched, and of course it is often what is happening now, these days, these moments, our troubles. But today my thoughts, which stayed all day and into my night and kept me awake, were about my love life. Or should I say the women who had entered my world. I'm no Lothario, really, I'm not. For so many years I was very shy around the opposite sex. I'm in my early 50s, follically challenged, and can be very introverted. I really could not see what others did. My old girlfriend, my true love, would ask me 'Why is that girl looking at you?' I would look around and ask, 'Which girl?' I really didn't notice. And I still don't see or get it. But the reality (I really don't want to appear vain) is that some do look, and even now there was more than one in my life. I was single and lived a fairly open life romantically. This journey was giving me an opportunity to think on the subject. I was alone, travelling for a couple of months, and I was determined to use this time to *put my house in order*.

In the past when I had got myself into situations like this, I had just cut and run and severed all connections. I'm not saying that was the smart thing to do, but it was my way of coping with the mess I created for myself. As I walked the decks and thought on this matter, I realised I would be doing the same, once again. Once I was home, maybe even before I reached there, before journey's end. And I don't say this in a light-hearted way. It's sad for all involved. No break-up is easy. I have the scars to prove it.

There was a girl from Taiwan in my life at that time, but really, where was that going to go? I wasn't moving to Taipei any day soon, and for sure, I was not asking her to move to London - I'm not even there most of the time.

It all changed back in 2006. Back at the time of my *big change*. I blame the Aegean Sea, the sun, that azure blue sea, and a newfound freedom and liberation from my former life. I blame it on my true love, my lost love. I blame it all on me. We are who we make ourselves become!

I never mean to hurt anyone, but I know I have, and that pains me. Pains me greatly. I find my way of moving on. I hope they can do the same; those wonderful people who filled my life for days, weeks, months and years. Those wonderful people I let down. Oh, yes, I carry some scars too.

Today was a day I would think about relationships, and it would be a long day. And a sleepless night, but by the morning I would feel calm and relaxed. I had also made some decisions, and the thing about making any decision is that it is better than making none. The Pacific was playing her hand again and again, and when I started to feel troubled, somehow, I found an inner peace. I calmed my troubled mind and steered a better path. She was helping me, the Pacific, in ways I could not possibly imagine. And tomorrow she would lay down her *Royal Flush*, and she would change me for good.

Day 30 Pacific Peace

When, on a day like no other, a day of surprise, peace finally filtrates like never before

"It's no use going back to yesterday, because I was a different person then." - Alice from Lewis Carroll's Alice In Wonderland

Lauryn Hill wrote, and sang, a great song, *"I Gotta Find Peace of Mind"*. Today I found mine.

The day started as those before on the *Hanjin Athens*, but it was to become a day I would never forget. A day that for reasons unbeknown to me, I would recall many times. A day which, and I'm not being overly dramatic when I say this, would change me forever.

Over breakfast, and for the one and only time, the captain asked me to join his table along with Vlad and the Chief Engineer Thomas. I felt like telling him to get lost, but instead I grudgingly accepted, and was ultimately glad I did. They asked a lot of questions about my journey and my life, and me equally of their existence at sea.

Vlad was on top form. I pressed on some of the port activities I had expected sailors to engage in - well at least the preconceived idea of such activities. Vlad didn't disappoint, he was very happy to open up about his *liaisons*, this being after the captain had left the table. It seemed that being restricted to ship, as we were in China, was not usual. In many ports, and providing off-loading and loading time permitted, the crew could *catch a break* and go ashore. He had me in stitches. Thomas had tales of his own but was a little more reserved.

I left that breakfast relieved that life at sea still offered a slice of the *old days'* adventure and fun. The sterility of what I had seen and understood had been dispelled a little, and for some reason that made me feel good. The idea of just sailing around the world for months on end in a comatose state didn't fit very well with me. The fact that from time to time the crew could let off a little steam seemed essential if a balanced equilibrium was to be observed. With Vlad, he almost lived up to the old saying, *a girl in every port*, if he was to be believed. And I believed, not because he was convincing, but because I wanted to.

The clocks went forward again today. I was now 10 hours behind London. Moving east, moving closer to home and counting down the time changes to Greenwich.

Today, for the first time in my life, I experienced a catharsis. And in so doing, I found a kind of peace I had previously not known. Martin Luther King, Jr., said *"Be The Peace You Wish To See In The World!"* I had not expected to travel halfway round the world to find mine, but find it I did - and since, I have tried to be the peace I want to see and be.

I spent the morning working through my now daily regime of study, reading and exercise, eventually going for lunch as usual around 1 p.m. No dining invitation, clearly breakfast was it for the day, perhaps the rest of the journey. So, after my post-lunch stroll, I returned to my cabin. Everything was normal, a little boring even. I got down on the floor to do some sit-ups, and suddenly I just stopped; sat up, and cried my eyes out uncontrollably for ten minutes. And after it was over, I laughed at myself and the onrush of such emotion. I felt a release, I felt good. Not that I felt bad before, but I just felt good. Calm, relaxed, at peace with myself, my surroundings, my life.

I had very little to worry about, at least no more than

any average middle-aged man with a couple of kids. I wasn't broke or ill. I didn't have relationship or family problems. As far as I knew, I wasn't headed into the stormy waters of a nervous breakdown. So quite why this release happened to me, I don't know. What was it? Deliverance, purging, relief? I didn't understand and in fact never have. I only know it happened.

I've often thought of that day and looked for cause. Was there a warning of what was to happen? But no, it just happened. What I can say, and with certainty, is that for years I have been *closed*. Others, close to me, have commented on this also, and for some years I was in denial, but with time I came to understand the truth. I built walls around myself, not to keep me in, but to keep others out. And whilst not ecstatic about this, it never really bothered me. That afternoon, just like Alice *In Wonderland*, I found a secret door. A door in my wall - and the Pacific had given me the key to unlock it.

I didn't know what to do with myself for an hour or so, I was in some kind of suspended state. I couldn't eat or drink, I was in a kind of trance - time meant nothing to me. Eventually I must have snapped out of it and found myself making circuits of the deck again. And I walked for some time, eventually going back to my cabin to get ready for dinner.

Upon my return to the real world, following my adventure, a few people commented on how healthy and relaxed I looked. And the truth was that I was both. Other than a bad couple of days at the start of my journey, I had not been ill or suffered, even though I was travelling in the winter months and had experienced some extreme climates. Yes, the journey had moments of anxiety and stress, but in the main I had remained calm. And on returning home, I never looked back at anything I had done in a painful way. My circumnavigation of the world was made in a relaxed and carefree manner. I sometimes think about those days, and my journey, as being made by someone else - as if I was looking at a TV show or reading a news article or book. An outsider looking in. It wasn't me that was travelling, I was just a voyeur looking in at myself.

I don't want to appear over-dramatic about this day. It happened, and I lived through it, and moved on from it. It's just that it never left me. Days in our lives are so many, and often forgotten. I mean the detail, unless they mark some important occasion, or offer an extreme of joy, drama or pain. I have those days like everyone, days I will never forget - but this day was something else altogether.

I think back to my time on the Pacific and understand that the peace I found is an enormously powerful thing, but it was not only about peace. Opening that door in my wall let others in, and before, that was not possible. I no longer have a wall or a door. I kept the key. I brought it back with me, and my peace of mind remains to this day.

Day 31 Pacific Rain

In which Phil starts planning for life after the Pacific

"If you want the rainbow you have to deal with the rain." -
Augustus

After the calm, the storm. Well, rain. It rained all day.
And as the day wore on, the tempest increased and the
seas turned rougher. The rain was joined by mist and for
the first time I felt cold, as a chill added to the worsening
conditions.

In a melancholy state, I started to think about
reaching the U.S. and what lay ahead travel-wise. I had
some time before my next ship would leave the east
coast for Europe, so intended to see parts of America I
had missed previously. I also had a tip from a friend to
get down to Mexico City, if time permitted. It did, so I
determined that as soon as I had internet access, I would
look for tickets south. I planned to base myself in Los
Angeles and go to Mexico from there and return to the
City of Angels to continue my journey and start my trek
across the country.

That was another part of this adventure that needed
some thought. I had enough days to go by car, bus or
train. Trains, again? But why not? So far, trains had
proved to be a very quick and reliable way to travel. So,
if there was a good option by train, all or part of the
way, I'd opt for it.

But with days to spare, I needed to think about
knocking off some of my wish-list. Chicago was top of
that list. I kept missing the Windy City and was
determined not to this time. So, I would look at options
that took me from L.A. to Chicago and then onward to
Wilmington.

Wilmington to Europe was pre-determined, as I would be heading off across the Atlantic from there in 22 days' time. The *MV Independent Voyager* was another container ship, and hopefully this time I would share the experience with some fellow passengers. In the meantime, I would arrive in Long Beach three days from now, so I would have 19 days to squeeze in the transit across the States, an excursion to Mexico and some days in Chicago. It all appeared doable.

In a masochistic kind of way, I had enjoyed my time at sea, but was beginning to feel the need to get on the move and explore. This 270-metre floating box was beginning to hem me in.

Day 32 Pacific Journey's End

In which Phil develops a greater understanding of what it takes to be a sailor, and where the motivation comes from

"I wanted freedom, open air and adventure. I found it on the sea." - Alain Gerbault

I was hardened to life at sea. But I would never become a convert; I would never become a sailor. I love the water, swimming, snorkelling and scuba diving, but I needed to get out of the water back onto dry land after an hour. Endless days sailing was no life for me.

Day 32 and I'm only halfway through my race around the world. It seems so much longer since I left London on that dark raining morning, heading to a London train station. Where was I now? On the Pacific. Just over halfway across the planet, just under half to go. London was a long way from here physically, and for me, mentally. That world, that life, so remote and distant from this.

I had travelled far and wide. I had covered our seven continents, and roughed my way near and far, but this... This journey, this was something different altogether. This was no beach resort or rucksack adventure. This felt like a mix of all that had gone before, and more, so much more. Yes, of all that had gone before, and all that would follow.

Frank, the cadet, found me some scales. I had lost six kilos in the past two weeks. My food intake had been steady, so the only contributing factor had been the volumes of exercise. Yet I knew this was an exceptional time and experience; I would never maintain such a routine when back in my normal life. We hear of actors rapidly losing weight to play a part, for example Christian Bale for the *Machinist*, but I'm sure he piled it back on - he certainly did for *Vice*! Just as I would; back to what passes as normal for me. Although I liked the new look, I also liked chocolate and ice cream, and sitting around reading books, listening to music and watching movies. So, chuffed as I was, it was a delusion, and I was savvy enough to know it. I decided to try and show some modicum of control for the next 32 days at least!

Sometimes strolling the decks, I would run into Karl. He dined in the officer's mess, but I was never sure of his rank. Whenever I saw him, he would have a paint pot in his hand, and would be painting a rail, or part of the deck; so, something to do with maintenance. He was outside in all weathers, and he invariably had a smile and friendly word for me.

In fact, no one appeared very miserable. I guess they knew what they were letting themselves in for before signing-on for each voyage. It was only me who had no idea whatsoever to expect. But I did next time, for the next voyage, for the Atlantic. I assumed that the salaries must be very high, to justify living such a life, however it is not really so. The average annual salary for an officer is US $40,000, and a captain averages US $80,000. I mean to say, there are waiters in the U.S. earning more in tips than ships' officers!

Tomorrow would be my last full day on board. I could see the light at the end of the tunnel. The promised land from somewhere over the horizon and beckoning.

Day 33 *Hanjin Athens* Final Day

Where the end of the voyage is met with a mix of emotions

"Once you have travelled, the voyage never ends." - Pat Conroy

And so, I come to the final chapters of life on the Pacific. Tomorrow we would arrive in America. Hamburgers and pizza awaited. Land. Firm, hard, solid land. No rolling sea, no swells, no peace. Life in America could hardly be described as peaceful.

The sun is shining again to herald our arrival. I am given another, a final, beautiful day to walk the ship. To live this strange life. The Atlantic waits. I imagine it will be *much of the same,* but I'm prepared for the next time on an ocean. I've lived through this one; I'm an experienced sailor now.

To my surprise Captain Schmidt invited me to his cabin to give my impressions of my journey on board his beloved vessel, his officers and crew. I played my cards quite close to my chest. Schmidt was no Ahab, but I wasn't going to give him any reason to *harpoon* me. I praised the food, the incredible experience, and kindness of all officers and crew. I apologised for the drunken night, God knows why, they were grown men, I hardly forced the booze down their throats.

As I sat there swooning over life on board, I briefly wondered what I would tell others. Well, I'm telling it, and I want to be as fair as possible. I had lived an experience very few had before me, and I suspect even fewer after. It had tested my reserves of patience. I had spent so much time alone, I had every right to feel lonely, but somehow, I hadn't. I have often reflected on this and questioned myself. I think that I kind of lost and found myself on the Pacific Ocean. The whole experience had seeped into me. I felt something deep inside, but I didn't understand it. It never left me, that feeling. Like the birth of a child, marriage, death... something happens to us, forces its way into us, never to be removed. Yes, I had travelled frequently, but sometimes I would return home and just think, 'Oh, that was a nice holiday.' Other times, something stuck. Like fishing in Broome, Australia with Aborigines, or standing under a glacier in New Zealand with my daughter. Imprints never to be erased.

The Pacific left imprints. The Atlantic very few. The first cut is the deepest!

I'm not sure travelling the Pacific as I did would suit everyone. There's the obvious risks of boredom and loneliness. But I think it's more than that. A certain state of mind is necessary. And the biggest problem is that once you cast off, there's no turning back. No jumping ship. It's a one-way ticket with no stops along the way. So, anyone thinking of following in my footsteps, be sure of what you are doing. I had had no idea. But whilst there were some uncomfortable moments, I know with all my being that I would not have missed this amazingly unique experience.

I spent my last full day following my well-honed routine. It was a beautiful day. The sun shone down on me as I walked, and I spent as much time as possible out there on deck for the last time. Me alone with the Pacific.

I had tentatively agreed to meet a couple of the officers in the evening. A farewell tipple perhaps? But no, true to form, socialising was not on this evening's menu. After a final dinner alone at my table, I went to the dayroom, and waited. And waited further, and finally returned to my cabin, and a DVD. *Gladiator.* You've gotta do what you've gotta do!

Day 34 Los Angeles and San Diego

In which ship is replaced by train, and not for the first time

"I travel the world, and I'm happy to say that America is still the great melting pot - maybe a chunky stew rather than a melting pot at this point, but you know what I mean." - Philip Glass

If it had not been for an American, I would not be arriving here today, and aiming to cross this vast land of opportunity, and conquer the world. Phileas is fictional, but Jules Verne based his character on the real-life adventurer William Perry Fogg. Fogg was a clever chap who wrote the Metropolitan Police Act of 1866, but his fame came from his travels around the world. A true inspiration for Phileas and Phil. In his first adventure he was one of the first Americans to travel through Japan and travelling west, eventually reached the Pyramids in Egypt.

The real Fogg kept journals and wrote of his adventures. His second book saw him travelling through Arabia to Baghdad. So, an American had reached Baghdad well in advance of the United Nations weapons inspectors. I wonder what he found in Iraq, way back in the 1870s, certainly no WMD, but then the UN never found any either! Like Fogg I had been to Baghdad, this in the 1980s and in the days when Saddam was flavour of the month with the Americans; he was waging war with the Iranians. One day friend, next day foe, it really is a funny old world! I remember going to a wedding in Baghdad and being asked to sing for the groom. It was a thing all foreigners attending were expected to do. The Japanese preceding me was booed off the stage. A German followed him - he lasted about 30 seconds. I went last; expectations were low, especially mine. I gave it my best shot and completed a rousing, mostly from fear (I was 24 years old), rendition of Daisy. They let me complete the song. With relief, I survived to wild applause. On returning to my table, at least 20 glasses of whisky had appeared. The rest of the evening was an understandable blur.

So, on a clear sunny morning, I had arrived in the homeland of Fogg, the forerunner to Phileas, who in turn was my inspiration. At 6 a.m. the *Hanjin Athens* docked at Long Beach container terminal, and my Pacific crossing was complete.

Waking to the realisation I would be leaving my floating hotel-prison filled me with mixed emotions. There is something about confinement that institutionalises us. Fortunately, I had not experienced prison, but hospitals, I had. And after a stay of four weeks in one when I was a young man, the feeling of leaving it to return home was similar to what I felt now. Apprehension. Red in the *Shawshank Redemption* had been institutionalised, and it nearly cost him in trying to adjust. Brooks had not been so lucky. Of course, my leaving the *Hanjin Athens* was nothing like as dramatic, but it did leave a strange uneasiness.

I had become accustomed to ocean life and the routines it brought. I had settled into my daily regime, adapted, and accepted it. And I had found an unexpected peace on the Pacific, that had permeated my soul. I would never forget day 30 of this journey and the effect it would leave on me for the rest of my life. And for that, and for the unforgettable, quite unique experience of crossing the Pacific, and in the manner in which I had, I would be eternally thankful.

So here I was, arrived in the New World, ready to get onto terra firma. Ready to head east, across this vast

145

continent to another, more violent ocean, and a passage home. I had booked myself onto another container ship; the *MV Independent Voyager*, which was to carry me across the Atlantic back to Europe. We would be sailing from Wilmington, North Carolina on day 53 of my journey, so this left me time to see parts of America I had missed. And even time for an excursion from and back to Los Angeles to continue my journey east.

Today, I would be heading to San Diego, also known as America's Finest City. Well, we would see about that! A couple of years earlier I had travelled with my son around Washington State and had the good fortune to stumble across Port Townsend, an amazingly charming little city that will be forever etched in my memory; so San Diego would have to really be something special.

After a quick, solitary breakfast, I went to see the U.S. immigration officer at the captain's quarters. He was amused at my reason for taking such an unusual entry into his country, but quickly processed me to be on my way. I was in no real mood to hang around and sought out those officers and crew who were available to bid farewell. The captain and his officers were all decked out in their uniforms for the arrival in port. I took a few snaps with them, collected my luggage and descended the gangplank I had staggered up a few weeks ago, to once again reach solid ground.

Time, as it so often does, had dragged and flown by at the same time. Wasn't it only yesterday I had waved goodbye to Hong Kong? The days had meshed into each other, and I had just gone with the flow, quietly biding my time, until this moment. I would again get into motion and move on with my quest. The ship had done her job. One ocean down, one to go. The peaceful Pacific would give way to the tempestuous Atlantic, and my stomach would be fully tested.

A shuttle took me to the port gate from where I grabbed a cab to Los Angeles. The taxi driver suggested he drop me at Fullerton train station where the Los Angeles to San Diego train would stop. When I off-loaded at Fullerton, I was immediately sceptical. There was no one on the platform and not even a ticket office. There was me, all alone, with my luggage for company. Perhaps the cab driver didn't fancy the ride into the city or was booked on another ride. Either way, I felt I had been taken for a ride myself, in every sense. But 20 minutes later, after contemplating taking another taxi, if only I could find one, I heard the unmistakable sound of a train approaching. After the number of trains I had ridden since leaving the U.K., I was becoming an expert!

Sitting comfortably heading to San Diego, I connected to the train's Wi-Fi and downloaded a stream of emails and messages. A couple from Sofia, my Trans-Siberian companion, jumped out at me, and I was relieved that despite quite a long recovery from an infection, she was on the mend. Her ailment and its cause would remain a mystery - it was a drama befitting such a momentous train journey.

I had so many mixed emotions flashing through my mind that I was unable to focus on many messages or the views out to the western coast. The ship and my time on her kept flashing back to me, as they still do to this day.

California was bathed in sunshine, the oranges would be ripening, and surfers getting ready to hit the peaks. Slowly the train made its way through numerous stops to downtown San Diego. It's one of the sunniest cities in America and was in its full glory for my arrival.

It's the eighth most populous city in the U.S. but had the feeling of being much smaller. A short stroll from the station had me in a hotel within easy walking distance to the Gaslamp district, my destination for the evening, and the waterfront.

It felt so strange to be surrounded by people. It was a glorious afternoon, and the waterfront boardwalk, cafes and bars were heaving. An unnerving sensation came over me and hit me like a physical force. I had to sit down to calm and compose myself. I found a quieter cafe and grabbed a late lunch on the waterfront. I still remember the Caesar salad and salmon and thinking what a massive change it made from the fare served up by the ship's galley. After a couple of glasses of chilled white wine, I felt more relaxed. But the wine would prove to be a mistake as it was shortly followed by numerous beers I was to share with a soon-to-be new buddy, Chuck.

Unbeknown to me, I had arrived on Super Bowl day. And to make matters worse, a Californian team, the San Francisco 49ers were contesting it. No wonder the place was so packed, and a palpable buzz was in the air. The Gaslamp district is a few blocks of endless bars and restaurants, and on such a day, gaining access was proving tricky. But I finally managed to blag my way into a bar and found myself next to Chuck, a very laid back but clearly impassioned 49ers fan. When asked, I naturally said the 49ers were my team. In fairness I had never heard of them and had no interest in American Football. Let's be honest, in the U.K. we play real football- soccer - and rugby - our equivalent of American football - but without the padded shoulders and helmets. But on proclaiming my loyalty to the 49ers, a beer arrived. It was to be the first of many, and on top of the wine and my meagre lunch, I soon started slurring and losing focus. Albeit for one drunken night on the *Hanjin Athens*, I hadn't drunk any alcohol for some weeks. So, knocking them back in a bar on the afternoon of the Super Bowl with all its heightened excitement was always going to set the conditions to get me plastered.

And get plastered I did, to such a degree that I have no recollection as to when I left that bar. I have no idea who won the game; and how I found my hotel I will never know. What I do remember is waking up in my bed in the middle of the night thinking I was on my bunk on the ship.

Day 35 San Diego

In which becoming a tourist for the day washes away some of the Pacific doldrums

"No matter where you are, you're always a bit on your own, always an outsider." - Banana Yoshimoto

Sleeping on land was proving harder than I imagined. Maybe I had missed my calling to sail the world's oceans. Life as a landlubber needed adjustment time. It hadn't helped that the hotel I chose was a dive. But the greatest influence on my insomnia had been the volumes of beer I consumed the evening before with my new buddy, Chuck, voracious fan of the 49ers, who after yesterday's Super Bowl result, was probably lying comatose somewhere if my throbbing head was something to gauge by.

One thing that Americans do, and do well, is breakfast. I threw my diet out of the window and went large on eggs, bacon and pancakes. Litres of coffee, which most Italians would spit out, was gratefully swallowed, and set me on my way. A long, lazy breakfast also set me up to wade through some of the many emails and messages that had built up over my time on the Pacific.

There was no external communication during my recent voyage, and in fairness I had not missed it. I quickly resigned myself to the fact that it would be many days before I would read an email or be able to call someone. But as I thought on this, I realised that throughout my journey around the world, so far, I had not called anyone since the dramas in Belarus and Poland. I don't think I sent any messages or emails either. I set out on this adventure wrapped in my own world as to what I was doing. And as I opened some of the many messages, I realised quite a few people had no idea I had left London.

That realisation would really hit me later when I looked inwardly at myself. My life. Considered how I lived, and how and who I was. Was I isolationist? I always felt that I was quite engaging with people, but I would come to question this. My childhood came flooding back, and I took a fresh look at what kind of boy I had been. Whilst reasonably friendly with others, even then I could see I was sometimes a little morose, or distant.

I am a quietly confident person. Considering my almost non-existent education, I had done reasonably well in life. Well enough to embark on a major life change in my mid-forties that enabled me to travel freely and share my time living in England and Greece. So yes, I am confident, and through my work had freely and successfully engaged with people at all levels and from all walks of life. But I was also self-determined, and if I'm honest, quite selfish. This single-mindedness has often uncomfortably rubbed shoulders with what I, and others, could consider as goodness. I consider myself a *good* person. But am I?

The sea gets in the blood, so it was no fluke that my planned tourist activities for today involved two ships; one to whale watch and the other a tour of an aircraft carrier.

Getting around San Diego was a breeze. I was staying close to the Gaslamp quarter and hung around there, Little Italy and Balboa Park. Everywhere I needed to be was within walking distance. And what a joy it was to exchange circuits of the *Hanjin Athens* for the waterfront and parks. I walked for hours in-between the sights, savouring every moment.

From previous numerous visits to the States, I considered the country a little unsafe, in larger cities, if you wandered too many blocks off the main drag. Some may say this is unfair, but it's what I have experienced when compared to European and Asian cities. I would only rate South America as riskier than its northern brother. I have always followed my instincts and feel when it's time to consider an alternative route. On a visit to Lima, I showed my map to the hotel concierge and asked where I should go. He put large crosses through 90 percent of the map. And having wandered close to some of those crosses, I would say he was giving his customers very sound advice.

In San Diego I didn't go wandering off the beaten track too much and felt safe the whole time I was there. But my unease definitely returned when I later reached Los Angeles, Chicago and Wilmington. I have a love-hate relationship with America, and most is love. The people are open and friendly and freely chat with visitors, often giving help as best they can when called upon. It really hurts me to still hold some negative thoughts and concerns.

As I made my way to the *USS Midway* aircraft carrier, which is now a museum, I remembered that *Top Gun* was set in San Diego. Maverick, Iceman, Goose and the rest of the gung-ho flyers must have had a ball in the Gaslamp district, if my brief indulgence was anything to go by.

Wandering around this massive ex-fighting machine, I was struck with many differing thoughts. One which has resurfaced on many occasions is that in this computerised technological age, so much of what I saw looked like it had come straight out of the World War Two era. The ship felt mechanical rather technological. This was perhaps a misconception on my part, but the thought didn't shift as I freely toured the ship. I later found out she had been commissioned shortly after that terrible war, so perhaps my reflection had been right.

The *Hanjin Athens* was big, very big, but this aircraft carrier felt like another scale altogether. Until 1955, the *USS Midway* was the largest ship in the world. But the reality is somewhat surprising. They are almost identical in size, with a few metres and tonnes difference. Phileas would have been shocked. The steamships he booked passage on for his journeys would have been no longer than 100 metres - three times shorter in length - and much smaller in tonnage. On the other hand, my compatriot would have been travelling in real style.

The *Midway* was impressive and strolling around, I reflected on the many conflicts in which she served - from Vietnam to the Arabian Gulf - the ship and her ever changing crew would have stories to tell that most of us could only realise in the movies. But many of us have seen her in the movies, as actual footage of a *F9F Panther* fighter crashing on landing was used in movies such as the aptly name *Midway* and *The Hunt for Red October*. The old bucket was famous, and I considered myself lucky to have had the chance to visit her.

My afternoon's nautical entertainment proved very different. I was going whale watching. Me and about 50 ship mates, heading out of port to find some whales. Having crossed the Pacific, this afternoon jaunt should have been a walk in the park. Not so; we bobbed and swayed our way in search of those elusive whales. A few revisited their lunch. Finally, after a couple of hours, and calls to return to port, our determined skipper spotted a couple of humps in the distance. We gave a distanced pursuit, but those humps moved off, and those lucky enough to have their cameras pointed and ready at the time of the first shout hopefully grabbed a few snaps.

One afternoon on the *Hanjin Athens* whilst losing myself on the gym's exercise bike, staring into the unending becalmed ocean, one of those majestic beasts had appeared, the sight of which had physically raised my spirits. But this day, rocking and rolling in the waters off San Diego Bay, I felt nothing of that majesty. We were unnecessary intruders on the migration of those wonderful beasts. A little part of me was happy we hadn't got closer, and happy that the humps soon disappeared when they realised that we were close by. But the shock, surprise and joy looking out of the gym's window that day would stay with me for ever.

I left my fellow sailors with a feeling that I wanted to be alone. I spent the rest of the day avoiding people. No more bars, getting smashed over a football game, no small talk. I silently enjoyed a quiet, early dinner along the waterfront, then made my way back to the Dive hotel, for an early night and hopefully long sleep. Tomorrow I would take yet another train and head to the City of Angels.

Day 36 San Diego to Los Angeles

Where Phil returns to Venice!

"I love Los Angeles. I love Hollywood. They're beautiful. Everybody's plastic, but I love plastic. I want to be plastic." - Andy Warhol

Today I return to Los Angeles for a brief stay before heading down Mexico way to visit the Capitalinos, at 2250 metres above sea level.

San Diego delivered the goods, and I was pleased I went the extra mile to see that little city by the sea. After a full American breakfast, and by full, I mean BIG, I was ready to hit the rails. Returning to Santa Fe station, I took a mid-morning train to Union Station, heading north along the coast and fully appreciating the sea views. The sun was shining, as it had throughout my stay; did it ever rain here?

The City of Lights was not new to me, and previous visits had shown me all the usual suspects. So, arriving at the impressive Union Station, part Art Deco, and part Spanish Colonial, I decided to head to the beach. The sea, once again, calling me. I had a short one night stay so thought that getting out of the city centre made more sense. As there was a direct bus to Venice Beach, I took that, and would work it out once I got there.

Almost everything about America is just like the movies, and LA is even more so than most places. The *Hollywood* sign up on the hill leaves you in little doubt what this place is all about. The bus was slow, taking two hours, but proved entertaining. The array of people that boarded and left was a real cross-section of the city and of American life. It was a bright sunny day and most I saw managed to put a smile on their face. Mexico was just across the border, and it showed. So many of those I saw had clearly come across to earn their dollar or join loved ones. Hispanics are the largest ethnic group in LA. What I saw, cruising that bus for two hours, was happy industrious folk going about their business. No gun-toting gangsters on every corner, as the movies would depict. Although in fairness, it was the middle of the afternoon, and we were heading towards the beach. Perhaps being in the West Adams or Skid Row districts wouldn't give the same feeling of safety. West Adams' crime rate was 500% higher than the national average! And, I suspected, the night would bring its own special brand of fear.

I sat on the bus thinking about that. About the night, and how a place can change. I had visited New York over the 4th of July one year, and along with 200,000 others had gone into Central Park to watch a concert. The setting was midway up and into the park. The show had started in broad daylight and ended after dusk, after one of the most impressive fireworks displays I have ever seen. I was staying south of the park so decided to stroll through it to reach my hotel. One minute I was surrounded by 200,000 smiling happy people, then suddenly as I headed south, I was all alone. The good folk of New York knew something I didn't and must have fled left and right for the nearest exit. I wasn't *Home Alone* for long, druggies crept out of the trees. No *Bird-Lady* for me. Seriously Kevin would not have ventured into that park alone in daylight, let alone night-time!

Finally reaching Venice Beach, I found a hostel offering room, breakfast and dinner for $70; it was a steal so I checked in. It was a block from the beach; I went for an evening stroll along the boardwalk. I was returning to the city in a few days, so this short stay was a stop-over before setting off for an excursion to

Mexico. I ate at the hostel and hung out with a few people there. Michel from Belgium was a good laugh, and we shared a bottle of red and swapped travel stories. He got nowhere near mine in Belarus and had to pay for the wine! Finally, I hit the sack, eager for the journey down to Mexico the following day.

Day 37 Los Angeles to Mexico City

When, after only four hours of travel, Phil enters a completely different world

"I was taken in by the bravado and the sounds of Mexico... not so much the music, but the spirit." - Herb Alpert

So many public displays of affection - couples kissing on every street corner. Just what lay ahead for me? If I had known it would be a Turkish tigress, I may never have boarded my flight to Mexico City. But I innocently took-off to another United States, *Estados Unidos Mexicanos.* I really only have myself to blame for what happened four days, and consequently four years, later.

Checking out of my hostel early in the morning, I made another booking for my return in five days' time. Nowhere could possibly match the price and location combination. Mexico was calling and nothing LA had to offer was going to keep me from heading down that way.

The taxi was big and brash, as was the driver, one vehicle encapsulating the *American Way.* Tony didn't stop chatting all the way down the coast, passing a concrete monster - Marina del Rey - to Los Angeles Airport - LAX. There were numerous apartment blocks gawking at the sea, and I was reminded of my bus ride through Repulse Bay on Hong Kong Island. *The World Is Just One Great Big Onion.* If only some of the words in that song could be taken a little more seriously. Trying to block out Tony, I wondered who would want to live in such monstrosities. Was this really the limit of how far ambition could reach? Surely there must be more?

LAX with its Theme Building, looking like something from a *Thunderbirds* set, fits right into the California vibe. Put that building in New York and it would stand out like a sore thumb; in LA it's like some far away alien universe found the perfect place to drop off one of its redundant spaceships. So here, in California, in Los Angeles, it fits right in. James Bond enjoyed some time here in *Moonraker*, and Al Pacino and Robert De Niro tore up the place in *Heat*. With Hollywood just up the road, it's little wonder the place is so popular as a movie set - the *A-Listers* could quickly be chauffeured home for cocktails after a hard day's work!

As I left the aircraft after a four-hour flight, I was gasping for air. It was like breathing through a straw. Was I back in Cusco, Peru? That was the last time I had this sensation - 2000 metres high, it took a few days to acclimatise before taking the *Inca Trail* to Machu Picchu - no I was arriving in Mexico City and had no idea how high it was!

Mexico City Airport is busy and arriving was a little over-powering. So many people crammed into such a small space! I was now an *anorak*; trains and ships were becoming my normal way of travel. My son will arrive at airports early just to *hang-around* in them - for me I wanted in and out as quickly as possible. And I was out of this one quick, far quicker than any American airport could spew me out. I mean, really, the airport immigration delays arriving in the U.S. can be horrendous. I missed a three-hour connection once whilst in transit, as I was obliged to enter the U.S. to then immediately leave it, though the same airport, ironically LAX!

No chit-chat from this Mexican taxi driver. And no comfort, with barely enough space for me and my small rucksack. Thankfully, I had left the bulk of my luggage at the hostel in Venice Beach. It's a short ride to the centre of the city; short in distance, long in time. The place was buzzing, people, cars and energy everywhere.

There are nine million people crammed into a place the same size as Los Angeles, but with more than double the population. Mexico City is the most populous city in North America, and it felt like it. And it was hot, very hot. From the freezing cold of Siberia to the sweltering heat of Mexico. My first stop would be to buy some flip-flops, my feet were melting in my boots!

I had booked a hotel before arrival. My mute cabbie dropped me outside and sped off into the afternoon crush, with a dozen car horns sending him on his way, having had the audacity to stop to let me out. I wasn't staying five-star, but it was clean, and the front desk were helpful. The room was massive, filled with heavy wooden furniture, and an en-suite in which I could swing a tiger. But more about tigers later! I dumped my things and headed out to find what the place was all about.

And what it was all about, was the people. People, people everywhere. There was a lot of passion openly showing itself. All those kissing couples, and a great deal of hugging and hand holding. Even elderly people were at it. Did they have no shame? Was it the heat that had induced such expressions of passion? I checked out this phenomenon, and read that Mexican men put their women on a pedestal - something to do with the Virgin Mary!

And, to balance all that love, the darker side; security guards on every shop front, and they were loaded and ready to defend the latest *Nike* sneakers. Busy streets and bustling shops. The place was alive. Ice cream is popular, as are tacos. Everywhere I looked people were licking at cones, and who could blame them? I was melting and the quicker I sorted out the footwear situation, the better.

I followed my nose down the main drag and ended

up in a massive square full of thousands of people. A few years later that square would feature as the opening scene for Bond's *Spectre*, a wild helicopter ride over the centre of Mexico City until Bond (inevitably) takes control. Now the square was full and there was no way through the crowd. I had no idea what was going on, but it looked fun and everyone was in high spirits. There were no skeletons, so I had missed the famous *Day of the Dead*. No, this was just a regular weekday. The place was already giving me a positive vibe.

Diving into a taco shop and picking up three very spicy tacos and a coke, all for one dollar, soon changed my mood. Boy, were those tacos hot! Within 30 minutes I was heading back to my hotel as fast as my clenched bowels would allow me. Those tacos were more than a match for the *currywurst* that had played havoc with me in Berlin.

Day 38 Mexico City

In which Mexico City weaves its magic and finds a new fan

"Thousands of Mexicans gathered in Mexico City to protest high food prices. The protest only lasted an hour, because everyone had to leave for their jobs in Los Angeles." - Conan O'Brien

I spent the day roaming the city. After waking early and half-heartedly attempting to continue my exercise routine of the *Hanjin Athens*, I checked some of the day trips out of the city on offer at the travel concession in the lobby. I booked two. I was turning into a tourist!

I walked, and walked, and never stopped. Wasn't Mexico supposed to be dangerous? I strolled around without a care in the world. Smiling people everywhere enjoying another startlingly sunny day. No threat of a drug cartel making a hit, or a child kidnapping. Denzel was here in *Man on Fire*, and he was getting that missing kid back, whatever the odds.

But I walked on and on, and no sight of anything untoward. Only happy, smiling people. I stopped from time to time for a drink or snack, but mostly just wandered around taking in the sights and the people - always the people - the colours and sounds and smells. Wandering into a park, there was some kind of festival going on, or maybe it was just normal life here. I found the inevitable taco vendor, and this time skipped the chilli sauce. Thankfully, no reaction. I decided to ignore my map for a few hours and see where I ended up.

Jesus appeared from time to time. Christianity showed itself on every street. One effigy a metre high was being paraded on a kind of plinth by four men. They set him down, and people emerged from shops and houses to put a few pesos in the collection box. That statue wasn't smiling, but perhaps it should have been, because it seemed to be raking it in.

The backstreets were awash in yellow, orange and other brightly coloured buildings. If it was to be believed, half the country was trying to escape to their northern neighbours; from what I saw, the other half appeared quite content where they were! How often did I see kissing and cuddling in LA? Never! If I had to stay in one of these two cities for any length of time, I would have to give the matter some serious thought. Kissing versus greed. For sure, both had their poor and needy, but the needy I was to later meet in Venice Beach could easily tip my decision and the scales in favour of *tacoland*. These mean streets also respected pedestrians. Yes, there were lots of cars, but they played second-fiddle to the shoppers. No scooters here trying to knock me down, as in Shanghai.

I needed the loo after all my drink breaks and found what looked like a shop offering me the opportunity to relieve myself for four pesos, about 20 US cents. There were rows of cubicles, I was directed towards one numbered '2' *caballeros*. The route to my stall took me across a bicycle and washing basket. It was surprisingly clean and fully functioning. I emerged onto the street to a pack of angry dogs. Was I in a scene from *Amores Perros*? No, these scruffy mutts were only looking for food and survival. This pack were no fighting hounds!

I was lost, but it didn't feel so. In fact, I felt right at home. I was wrapped-up in my own world, well… their world. Alone, but surrounded by so many. I didn't speak to anyone, but I did smile quite a lot, and they smiled back. They probably wondered what the hell I was doing there. I don't recall seeing any other *gringos*.

It wasn't just the buildings that were colourful, the

163

locals were dressed in every type of multi-coloured clothing imaginable. It definitely added to the *happy* feel of the place. And if you want to find real cowboys, Mexico has more than its fair share. In fact, that is true of most of Central America. A few years later I would encounter so many of them as I travelled through El Salvador, Honduras and Nicaragua. And those cowboys loved their horses, often riding them into their local towns to parade on a Sunday afternoon. Central America often gets a bad rap, but like so many places in the world, there is far more good than bad.

The churches are very impressive; filled with golden statues and altars. No expense spared in Mexico's show of devotion. There must have been large amounts of pesos being collected in those boxes. Not as opulent as in Peru and Ecuador, but still these churches were more extravagant than their counterparts in Europe. I took respite from the sun in one of those golden palaces and rested my hot swelling feet. My boots had been exchanged for some knock off Havaianas, but they were still suffering from the relentless heat!

By mid-afternoon, I had alighted from my wandering at the city's angel: The Angel of Independence was shining her gold over the city. As a boy I had chosen (for no reason) Mexico for a school project, and unlike most of my schooling, I had some enthusiasm for this project - I have no idea why! I got top marks - the one and only time. Mostly school passed me by, and it's fair to say, I did not excel at anything. In fact, quite how I have made such a good life for myself, I will never know. Taking risks! 'Thanks, Dad.'

It's funny what we remember from our childhood, what gets stuck and rears itself. Mexico hosted the Olympics in 1968. I remember that. And I remember the black men kneeling with a black-gloved fist raised in salute. At the time I had no idea why. I was nine. But those men and gloves appeared many times on the winner's rostrum and appeared many times to me over the years. I remember watching a man fly at those Olympics. He just flew through the air, and when would he land? Bob Beamon was my Mexico City Olympics hero. Me and almost everyone else! And now, here I was in Mexico. The land of my school project. The land of peaceful protest. The place where a man flew. Yes, I was very happy I had eventually made it to Mexico. Very happy indeed.

Checking my map, I slowly headed in a direction towards my hotel. The sun was slowly setting, but the city held one more treat for me. I stumbled upon The Monument to the Revolution. It wasn't the monument that impressed itself upon me, but the water spouts in its plaza. Jets of water gently shooting upwards, and children frolicking in them, trying to cool off or just having fun as they got drenched. I was so hot I nearly joined them!

I eventually collapsed onto my enormous wooden bed and took a late siesta. Rousing myself, the sun had set and venturing out into the still hot evening, the city was coming into another kind of life. People milling around everywhere, eating and drinking. Music drifting out of cafes and bars filled the already heightened atmosphere. It's little wonder so much love was in the air.

Day 39 Mexico City Pyramids

In which Phil is transported back to another land of pyramids

"The Aztecs believe they started up in what's now New Mexico, and wandered for 10,000 years before they got down into where they are now, in Mexico City. That's a weird legend." - Jerry Pournelle

Pyramids, not Egyptian, but Mexican. Aztec. As a small boy I remember my father climbing to the top of one in Giza. That was in the 60s and we were visiting my Greek grandmother who was living in Cairo at that time. My twin, Dave, was riding a camel. I, being too scared by the beast, was on a donkey. Brave Dave was always stronger than me. We have a photo of Dave, my sister Claudia and me, each standing on a stone of a pyramid, a ladder to the summit with my dad, disappearing into the clear blue skies, climbing up that pyramid. They would probably shoot you if you tried that trick today. Those precious sacred resting places of the pharaohs are not to be clambered over if they are to survive another 4,500 years.

I was climbing a pyramid, an Aztec one, and no one was shooting at me, and a few hundred other tourists were joining in. A few years from now they would probably stop us, just like those clever Egyptians. But, on another sunny day I made my way up that pyramid into the clear blue sky just like my dad had.

I booked myself onto a full day tour out of the city to Teotihuacán. A minibus collected me at my hotel at eight in the morning, and we did the rounds, loading about ten others. They were all South American tourists, in from Chile, Peru and Colombia. And a fun bunch they were too, especially the Colombians, who took me in as one of their own. Their names are lost to me now, except Sandra, who remained in contact for some years.

On the way to the pyramids, we stopped at South America's holiest place, and for me the highlight of the tour. The Basilica of Our Lady of Guadalupe houses a shrine and is an impressively large 1970s round building. From outside it could pass for a small stadium or concert hall. But once inside there's no mistaking the ecclesiastical vibe. I was blown away by its size, and the overall feel. It was cavernous, and very 70s, with a snake of suspended lighting hanging down over marble floors. The place was swarming with people, all eager to see the cloak of Juan Diego. Shrines have existed at the site since the fourteenth century, and the story goes that the Virgin Mary presented herself to Saint Juan Diego. His cloak had been imprinted by winter roses with her image. And that cloak hangs as the focal point of the basilica.

Someone planted a bomb in the basilica and tried to blow up that cloak back in the 1920s - the bomb exploded, but a higher power ensured that the cloak survived.

Millions visit the basilica each year - only the Vatican receives more visiting Catholics - and whilst I'm not religious (I would say I have *faith*, even if I do not know what in), the place held me in awe. I was told a story of some scientists testing the cloak, and being amazed that it retains its colours, which are still so vivid. It's beautiful and held me in its power for some time. I would reflect later that day that it was the basilica and the cloak, and not the pyramids, that was the highlight. The building, devoted crowds, and of course, cloak, often return to my memory.

We moved on to Teotihuacán, me and the South

Americans, and one of them was getting fruity. And if the truth be told she was quite attractive, Sandra was showing me some interest. Normally I'm not very good at noticing the signs, but they clearly do things differently in Colombia, and these signs were flashing neon, their message loud and clear.

Nudging our way through the heavy traffic, we eased out of the city. The Volkswagen Beetle is an icon, and they abound in Mexico. And I'm speaking of the original air-cooled version, not the modern plastic remake. The Mexicans were still producing them up to 2003, long after we gave up in Europe. Hitler was a bad man, we all know that, but let's give credit where it is due - he was responsible for the commissioning of the VW Beetle. And who knows, perhaps he drove one for years after his war, hiding out with his pals in South America!

The Beetle holds many memories for me, as my father drove one throughout his life. My first memories of being in a car were in a Beetle, and that continued until I left home and bought my own car. On a trip to the coast once we squeezed a family of five, our luggage and a caged budgerigar into one! *The People's Car* it certainly was.

In Mexico City they are used as taxis, with the front passenger seat removed to enable loading of up to three or more passengers on the back one. I rode one before leaving the city - a red and gold beetle crawling over the sun-baked tarmac, taking me around the city and back to my childhood.

The Aztecs didn't appear to have the head for heights of their Egyptian pyramid building counterparts. Or perhaps their gods were not so revered. Whatever the reason, the Mexican versions were lower, and therefore much more accessible. The highest, Pyramid of the Sun, at 75 metres, was less than half the height of The Great

Pyramid of Giza, and I was thankful as I drifted away from my fellow tourists to climb it. Reaching the top, the view of the Teotihuacán site was spectacular. Multiple ruins spread over very flat land, ringed by greenery and mountains in the far distance. Those poor souls, those chosen ones, had to hike up some 200 steps just to get their heads lopped-off in sacrifice. But if you've got to go, this was a very pretty place for it!

Over a late lunch, I got to chat and ask about the lives of the group. They were extremely friendly and loved to laugh and joke around. More photos were taken of us, in different formations, than of the pyramids. It was like being at a Thai wedding! I always think of South Americans as being poor, so I guessed Sandra and the others were relatively affluent to be vacationing in Mexico. But, who knows, maybe they saved up for this trip. One thing is for sure, they were sure having a good time.

From my experience, wherever you were in the world, if you took a tour, you would probably be served salad, rice and chicken for lunch. Mexico proved to be no exception. But this is Mexico, so some beans and salsa were added to spice things up a little. After lunch, there was a final look around and a small lecture on Aztec history and we were on our way back to the city. Every tour you take anywhere in the world will eventually bring you to some kind of shopping outlet. I guess with Mexico's northern friends coming down in their droves, shopping was one of the highlights. Didn't those wealthy Americans realise the prices were inflated to take into account the additional commissions that would be paid out?

I wandered around the gift shop with little enthusiasm to buy anything. Frida Kahlo's face appeared on a wide assortment of items, from mugs to tea towels.

I would be visiting her house tomorrow, so could catch up with such goodies then. I wonder what she would think of her sad face being plastered all over that tourist merchandise? I would like to think it would make her sadder and not happier.

We finally moved on, back to the heart of the city, and took the reverse route to drop off us weary tourists. An hour in that cramped van snuggled up to Sandra was more than enough romance for me. Lovely as she was, she wasn't my type. As they alighted at each hotel I bade farewell, and finally reached mine. I was tired but very pleased to have made the tour and experienced for that brief time the Aztecs, and most of all, the bomb-blast surviving cloak with its rose imprinted image of the Virgin Mary.

Day 40 Mexico City Frida

In which the bluest blue rubs off leaving the bluest of blue days

"I tried to drown my sorrows, but the bastards learned how to swim, and now I am overwhelmed by this decent and good feeling."
- Frida Kahlo

Bristol ultramarine blue of a vibrancy to put a smile on any face. That's the colour of Frida Kahlo's house in Mexico City, and as I waited in an eager queue to enter and pay homage, I was smiling. I had been smiling all morning, and I had no idea why.

I took breakfast in a busy little cafe across from my hotel. Coffee - no tea to be found in this city - so when in Rome! So, coffee and *churros*, I was in heaven. Those Mexican doughnuts were fresh, crispy, soft centred, sugar-coated heaven. Over a foot long, I managed two! It was my second time in this cafe and already I felt like a local, recognising those regulars around me. How quickly we blend in, form habits, and then become anonymous. At a cafe in Chianni in Tuscany on my second morning I had coffee and croissant delivered to my table before I could order. I stayed a few more days, and never ordered.

The Metro in Mexico City is wonderful. Clean, efficient and with wide coverage across the far corners of the city. Colour everywhere. No drab greys like Siberia in this part of the world. No heavy coats and fur-lined boots; no complaining about the lack of a Metro here, just sunny, happy, T-shirt clad people moving around the city earning their pesos. And they only need three pesos to take a ride to any destination.

I alighted and walked a little in the Coyoacán district

until I found my destination. The Museo Frida Kahlo. The clue was in the name! That tragic artist had lived here, on and off, with husband Diego Rivera from 1929 until 1954. Until her death, aged 47. But she had lived at La Casa Azul (The Blue House) since early childhood. So, it was her family home. Diego had muscled in! She was one of those famous people that died young, later, after death, to become an icon. Death too soon... maybe it's a factor in their fame, or infamy. Jimmy Hendrix, Che, JFK, them and so many, gone before their time, and becoming immortals. I'm not putting Frida in the same category as JFK, but her image, like Che's, is global, and will be long remembered after many others have come and gone. As an artist, she wasn't so famous in her lifetime. Her first solo exhibition was the year before her death, the year she had a leg amputated. Solo leg. But then look at Vincent - solo ear - exchanging art for food, simply to survive. He would be laughing his other ear off if he knew what one of his paintings went for now. Is art valuable because it's good, or because a select few decide it is? This question has always troubled me.

The bluest of blue walls announce your arrival at the right place, long before you reach the *museo*. I was queuing in the *Calle Londres* and felt right at home. Me and few dozen others, eager to enter Frida's world and learn more about this enigmatic woman. The house did not disappoint. The volume of artwork did. I guess it was distributed to galleries and private collections around the world. The house was quite simple, but totally charming.

I wondered as I walked around if the bright colours of blue, yellow and red adorned the place during Frida's years here, or if someone had thought that commercially they would add to the charm. Certainly, the outside was blue, just consider the name. I like to think that as tragic and short as her life was, it was filled with colour.

There was a time when Diego Rivera was one of the most famous artists in the world, but Frida certainly trumps him these days, and her reach extended much further after the widely successful movie, *Frida* starring Salma Hayek. I would rewatch that movie upon my return to *Londres*.

My art juices were flowing. I took the Metro to Chapultepec Park, for a visit to the Museo de Arte Moderno. As expected, Frida and Diego feature, along with many fine South American artists. But there was something about the place that didn't fit with me. I felt a little blue. Perhaps it was Frida's house invading me? Perhaps I had been seduced by the intimacy of that much smaller *museo*, and its painful history? I didn't hang around long and set out to walk back to the downtown district. A very long hot walk that left me with an increased, enhanced, positive feeling about Mexico. Eventually I turned into my hotel street, exhausted but fulfilled by such a wonderful day.

Day 41 Mexico City Taxco

Which doesn't go exactly according to plan

"In Mexico, everything on the menu is the same dish. The only difference is the way it's folded." - Billy Connolly

Finally, I was living *Groundhog Day*. Well at least it felt like it. I was on another minibus doing the rounds, collecting tourists. But unlike the *pyramid* day, my fellow day-trippers were a real assortment of ages and nationalities.

I fell asleep in the bus. Last night, as tired as I was, I ventured out for a quiet and early evening. Things hadn't gone according to plan. Tonight would put last night in the shade!

Yesterday evening after crashing for an hour, I had gone out to grab a bite to eat and walked into a 20,000 plus crowd packed into the main plaza and streets leading into it. There was a live open-air concert, and it felt like half of the city had come out to join in the fun. The happy people of Mexico City had stepped-up a gear and this party was going to go on long after I was counting sheep.

So today I was sleep deprived; after what felt like an hour, the minibus suddenly stopped, and I was jolted awake. I woke, to find an elderly Canadian lady squeezed in next to me. Jean took the occasion of my waking to tell me her life story. It beats me why so many people are prepared to impart so much of their lives to complete strangers. Jean was one of those people who could be everyone's grandmother! She introduced me to her friend (who she had met the previous evening), Zeynep. That's not her real name, and as our story unfolds, no one will blame me for changing it. Zeynep was in her late thirties, and an accountant from Ankara in Turkey.

Small, slim, and quite attractive. And she seemed so sweet and innocent, and this misconception is responsible for what would follow.

We were headed out of the city to a couple of mountain towns, firstly Cuernavaca, and then on to Taxco to visit the famous cathedral. Fate would play its hand and I would never see the inside of that cathedral, as I got stuck in a bar all afternoon drinking cheap Mexican beer. This is a shame, as Taxco Cathedral is apparently amazing; it is famed for having the only icon of a pregnant Virgin Mary.

I'm getting ahead of myself, because Cuernavaca is worth a mention. It's a beautiful colonial town, and my new acquaintance, Diego Rivera, would rear his head in the form of some murals in one of the two tourist haunts, the Palace of Cortés. The second, and more impressive in my opinion, is the Cuernavaca Cathedral, housed in a 1500s walled monastery. Its simple stone facade belied the arched beauty inside. It was very plain, especially when compared with so many gold-laden churches in Mexico; but perhaps it was the simplicity that made it all the more appealing. The gardens offered a beautiful luscious green respite from the baking heat of the late morning sun.

We stopped for lunch and shopping at a silversmith. The Taxco region is the silver capital of Mexico. Taxco Cathedral was built by a wealthy silver baron - presumably, he was eternally thankful for his good fortune. There was a lot of silver on display, and Jean, an equal match for her cousins in South America, was eager to off-load some dollars.

And so eventually we arrived in Taxco proper. The main square on which the cathedral sits was as vibrant as anything I had seen in Mexico. Cobbled streets surrounding a small park at its centre. Restaurants and many bars had terraces overlooking the square and cathedral. And after a long sweaty drive they were too inviting. Zeynep and I popped into one for a cooling beer. And there we stayed. I ordered some food as I skipped the lunch. The menu confused me as I had no idea what the difference was between *Tacos, Tortillas, Quesadillas* and many other options. We ate, we drank, and we stayed. And then stayed some more. Eventually our guide spotted us and shouted up that the bus was leaving. I'm not sure how long we were in that bar, but do I know we missed the cathedral tour, and I never got to see the pregnant Mary! I remember giant puppets parading below us making a couple of circuits of the square as we supped beer after beer, but little else.

The journey back to the city was something straight out of a school trip cliché. We took over the back seat. The ride was a bit of a blur, as was the rest of the evening. What I can say without any hesitation was that at the time I had no regrets - I can also say that what was to follow four years later has haunted and filled me with many.

Taxco, and my day trip out of Mexico City holds many memories for me, but none have anything to do with a cathedral, a pregnant Madonna, or silver!

Day 42 Mexico City to Los Angeles

In which Phil escapes to live another day, and heads north back to America

"That's the funny thing about trying to escape. You never really can. Maybe temporarily, but not completely." - Jennifer L. Armentrout - Onyx

I asked, 'When was the last time you made love with a man?' She answered, 'Four years ago.' I knew I was in serious trouble.

That was four years in the future, now in Mexico City, I woke in a totally disorientated state. For the briefest of moments, I thought I was paralysed. My legs wouldn't move. I quickly realised they, and I, were pinned to my bed; and I equally quickly realised by what, or I should say who.

Zeynep (the some-years-later-to-be-named Turkish Tiger), had stayed the night. *Oh, What A Night...* I must have crashed-out at some point, but as the cold light of day cleared my head, it all came flooding back to me.

I was due to leave Mexico City this afternoon and resume my stay in America and ultimately my journey across the *Land of Opportunity* to my destiny with the Atlantic Ocean; and return to England. So, I did not have time to hang around. Gentleman as I am, I offered Zeynep breakfast at my now regular coffee shop. And after that, I bade a relieved farewell to her. She was nice, let me go as far as to say sweet, but there was a desperation about her that was unsettling. The truth was what had happened was for one night only. Or at least that's what I thought at the time!

We stayed in email contact, me and Zeynep. Annual exchanges and pleasantries at Christmas. I guessed with time they would just fizzle out. I certainly never expected to meet her again. But I was oh so wrong on that count. Somewhere along the way I must have mentioned where I lived in Greece each summer. Stupid of me really, because I know enough about geography to know that where I live is only a hop-skip-jump from Turkey. It must be because a flood of refugees regularly piled into rubber dinghies to reach the promised land of the European Union in that region.

One frantic summer afternoon, my dog, Belaki, had gone missing. She had just wandered off, and not for the first time; but today she was missing all day. I blame her, Belaki, for the mess I got into with Zeynep. In a state of near panic, I was scooting around the island looking for the missing mutt. After a fruitless, sweaty hour, I returned home. I was hot, bothered and stressed. As I was going up the stairs to my house, I saw a small figure in a large hat walking up my driveway. I stopped and looked. From a distance I had no idea who was coming to visit. The hat drew closer and was removed to reveal, you guessed it, Zeynep. Now ordinarily this should not have caused me much concern. However, a female *friend,* Ciara, was staying on the island at the time, and occasionally *visiting* me. Plus, I had a missing Belaki to consider.

I was in shock but managed to calm down and establish some facts. Zeynep was only staying one night. Yes, she assumed she could stay with me. Yes, she appreciated that we had not agreed to this visit, but she was in the region. I didn't believe her. No, she wouldn't be any trouble, she promised. Her ferry was leaving at 6 a.m. the following morning. Having taken stock of the facts, I decided to buy myself some thinking time; I scooted off again in search of the missing Belaki. After 30 minutes, I found her in the port about to be kidnapped by a middle-aged Italian couple who were on a yacht. I went ballistic with them. Retrieving her and returning home, I was filled with a mixture of relief and euphoria. That euphoria led to events that were to result in a friend of mine later that evening naming Zeynep, The Turkish Tiger. One thing led to another and to this day I swear she took advantage of my emotional state because of my dog. Eventually I managed to escape around 9 p.m., saying I had a prior appointment I couldn't miss and would return by midnight. I was in shock when I met a couple of friends for dinner. And when they looked at my scratched arms they were also in shock, until I told them what had happened, and then they were in hysterics. Ciara showed up at the restaurant and asked if we could meet up later. 'NO!' I almost screamed at her. I made my apologies, saying we were celebrating a friend's birthday. We weren't, but it was the best I could come up with at short notice. I promised I would come down to the port the next morning to say goodbye. Unfortunately, that was a promise I knew I could never keep!

I returned home at 4:30 a.m., sober as a judge, irrespective of how much I had drunk. The Turkish Tiger was waiting in my bed. I put on my best acting performance ever, pretending to be drunk as a skunk as I slipped into bed and fought off her advances. Clever chap that I can sometimes be, I had set an alarm for 5:30 a.m. to ensure she didn't miss her ferry. That was the longest hour of my life. Longer than those I suffered crossing Poland! I lay fully awake pretend snoring as she clawed at my back. And when I say that girl knew how to claw, I mean it. I had a number of scars that took weeks to heal. Physicals scars; the mental ones took longer.

The alarm finally sounded, and I roused myself and

managed to get her on my scooter to take her to the port. The next problem was that Ciara would be there, as she was taking the same ferry! I, within sight of the port acted, what really was, Oscar-worthy stuff. I stopped the scooter and said I was going to throw-up. I asked her to walk the rest of the way to the port, to be sure she didn't miss the ferry. With a look of concern for me, she hugged me goodbye. I returned home, sat collapsed onto the bench on my terrace; looking down to the port I watched that ferry come in. When it departed five minutes later, I was praying that they both got on it. And here's the thing, I had no guilt or remorse at my shocking behaviour, even though I know the blame for the entire mess was all mine.

It's fair to say that I can now look back and laugh at this ridiculous situation, but at the time I was completely spooked. I wrote to Zeynep a month after her surprise visit to Greece, telling her I had met someone and planned to get engaged to marry. Utter twaddle, but it worked. She never showed up again, and the messages and contact ended. There was a lesson to be learned from this whole experience, but I was pretty sure I would not learn it! Time proved me to be right on that one.

So, on a sunny Mexico morning, I hailed a taxi to take me to the airport; and I allowed time for the heavy traffic. I was still in some kind of daze from the previous 24 hours, so the journey back to the U.S. is retained in my far-away sub-consciousness.

Mexico City had exceeded all my expectations, and then some. The place was alive in every sense of the word. I had well and truly shaken off the Pacific blues. Sailing the Pacific, when was that? It felt like it happened months before, not a week ago.

Eventually I was back at Venice Beach; reunited with

my luggage, and eager to take a cold shower, and have a very early night before hitting the tracks (literally) the following afternoon.

Day 43 Venice Beach and Amtrak

In which Phil tries to shake off the romance of yesterday to see the potential of today!

From the movie:
"Have there been any women in his life?" - Princess Aouda asking of Phileas Fogg
"I assume he had a mother, but I am not certain." - Passepartout

Today, I resume my journey and quest to beat Phileas at his own game. Once again, a long train journey awaits to carry me to the Windy City. I've looked forward to reaching Chicago, a city I barely know, determined to change that situation.

Trains and more trains… I wonder, yet again, why such a trouble-free mode of transport has passed me by. My planned journey starting today would be three days trundling across the New World in the kind of luxury that the Russians and Trans-Siberian Railway management could learn a lot from.

But first, the morning held a nice surprise in the form of Donna. And again, I would be presented with one of those opportunities in life, and during this journey in particular, that would make me question whether I should be boarding a train or not.

I checked out of the hostel, leaving my luggage to collect later before heading off to Union Station. Venice Beach is exactly as you see in the movies. At any moment you could expect to see a poodle skateboarding down the promenade or a geriatric lifting weights at one of the outdoor gyms. The sun was shining and the place buzzing. I headed out across the beach, along one of the jetties stretching into the sea, probably the one that would later feature in *La La Land*. I'm no Ryan Gosling, but the day would soon prove that there was still some charm in the old dog.

Walking along the Venice Boardwalk, I drifted back a few years to a previous visit, and again reflected on the change that has afflicted a place. There is still the buzz, but there is more threat in the air. Less spirit. The winter months attract many homeless from all over the States. I stopped and spoke to one, Greg, originally from Denver. Greg looked like he was in his 60s but was only 45. He was *vacationing* to avoid the winter months. He had lost his job, and like so many in this land of opportunity, was a *nomad,* moving from place to place. Sometimes catching some cash-paid work, mostly not. California offered him very little, other than the chance to not freeze to death on a winter's night. The place was full of Gregs, as had been San Diego. Nomads sleeping rough or living in their cars. One in eight Americans lives in a trailer. For Greg and his fellow sun-seekers a trailer would appear like a palace.

But America is nothing if it isn't extreme: for every Greg there is an *affluent* living in a swanky, waterside, designer home. Although the scales were clearly tipping numerically towards the Gregs, some of the homes looked amazing. Boxes on poles floating in the clear blue skies; mirrored walls giving the illusion of a second ocean. They were all there, along with the medicinal cannabis stores and vegan cafes. The rich were having a ball and loving the skinny lattes, the poor enjoying living another day, happy to sup some suds, both soaking up the Californian sun.

Los Angeles had it all, miles of sandy sunny beaches. The City of Angels, California, U.S.A., The World. Sprawling and brazenly flexing its muscles to the rest of humanity. Oranges, money and Hollywood. The place

183

had it all in swathes - it had every right to boast and boast big. I mean, California has an economy larger than Germany's! All the young men had gone west, and now the homeless too.

With time on my hands, I wandered along, passing the Muscle Beach gym; I wasn't sure if I was in awe, frightened or found the sights too hilarious for words. There was more testosterone on display than you would find in the whole of New York city. I wandered along the beach pathway in the direction of Santa Monica Pier. Enter Donna. I saw this vision of beauty walking towards me along the path. She was Michelle Obama's younger sister, but with even better looks. Looks to die for. It was a movie scene, right there in the place of so many, I was making my own. As we approached, I smiled, she smiled, I walked on and looked back as she looked back. We walked towards each other. Yes, it sounds like a script, it should be a script, but it wasn't. It was real, and I was suddenly lead in a Hollywood *rom-com*.

She was an actress heading to an audition later that afternoon. I was an English adventurer, travelling the world, attempting to beat the record of a famous fictional character. More Hollywood script - really you couldn't write this stuff. And boy was she beautiful, she made Maja from Poland look like the ugly sister.

We decided to stroll to the pier, chatting as we did so. It felt like the most natural thing in the world. Walking along with her at my side, telling our stories. I grew about a foot taller just being in her presence. What a smile, look, character. She was the complete package. Where was her leading actor? Amazingly she didn't have one. Enter me, the Englishman, with a train to catch in 3 hours for a long-haul across America to minus four degrees and snow. Was this history repeating itself? Was

I really going to take that train?

We took photographs under the *Santa Monica 66 End of the Trail* sign. Forrest Gump and Cinderella. Tom had been there before turning around and heading back east. Tom, and many others had stood where I stood, and now it was my time, Phileas Phil. And like Tom, I was planning to turn around and head east. East to Chicago and the Atlantic and home.

But Cinderella was staying here in Sunnyville, California so why would I even consider skipping town? I took a photo of Cinders with the famous Ferris wheel behind her. My next photo in sequence is of Los Angeles Union Station which can only mean one thing!

I look at those photos, in sequence, from time to time and wonder at the gap; the three hours between the two shots, Ferris wheel and train station. As Anohni from Antony and the Johnsons sang, *"We live together in a photograph of time"*.

Again, I found myself standing on a station platform eyeing an enormous snake of a train stretching as far as I could see. It could have been the train from *Silver Streak*, the comedy murder movie set on a train on this route. I wondered what lay ahead, would I find Gene Wilder and Richard Pryor on board? The *Southwest Chief* was taking me from Los Angeles to Chicago and she was leaving in 15 minutes. It would take three days to reach our destination, and there would be a lot of time for reflection on what had been another extraordinary day. We pulled away on schedule at 6:15 p.m. precisely and I bade a sad farewell to Los Angeles, San Diego and Mexico. It would be fair to say my days had been full and my life full of fun and the unexpected since I had disembarked the *Hanjin Athens*. Those peaceful days circling the ship's deck, staring into the vast emptiness of the Pacific had been followed by a roller-coaster of activity. I waved goodbye to Hollywood and my time as a real-life film star.

What lay ahead was a journey through eight American states on an Amtrak train which would chug along 24 hours a day, stopping 31 times along the way, at stations from Albuquerque to Dodge City.

The *Southwest Chief* was no *Orient Express* and thankfully not a *Vostok*, but it was big welcome to America, and comfortable, just like American motor cars. It had an observation lounge and a wonderful dining carriage. Without time restrictions, it was a great way to cross and see some of this enormous country in luxury. Sure, the freedom of the road was missing, but so were the hours of cruise control and highway diners.

I had booked a sleeping compartment and fully inclusive dining service. Taking everything into account, I would argue it was the best value for money on my entire journey. At U.S. $400 it was worth every cent. My compartment was small but pleasant. The car attendants would make up my bed whilst I dined in the evening and clear it way over breakfast.

Again, I would be without Wi-Fi, which after the Pacific crossing would be a doddle, and I had anyway not missed the interruption of daily electronic communication. But the *Chief* did not offer isolation, in fact far from it. It was clearly a popular route, with a mixture of those scared of flying, travellers, business people and families. There would be an ebb and flow as we reached stations along the way. The most consistent group, who were going *all the way*, were from the Amish community. Flying was out of the question for them, so they took the train to Chicago then transferred down to Pennsylvania. I would get to meet a few along the way, and it made for interesting times.

Over my first dinner, four Amish were at the next

table. I had never encountered these people before, so upon seeing them was immediately transported back to *Witness*, where Harrison Ford is hiding out amongst their community. I had gone from the homeless in Venice Beach, to an actress on Santa Monica Pier to Kelly McGillis. This was for sure a very diverse country, and I was realising it, hour by hour. There were days on this journey that flew by, especially those at sea, with their monotony. But days like today seemed to fill a week. I was living days to the full and after, I would look back and think that 65 days had felt like 165. I was seeing and doing so much. Meeting so many different and fascinating people. Traveling sure throws up some interesting characters.

I dined with an elderly couple. Quite distracted, my thoughts drifted back to Santa Monica Pier, but the subject of yet another mass shooting came up, and I was dragged back to the present by this topic. They were a homely couple, Fred and Sue, so I was surprised, when I asked how they felt about the availability of guns in their homeland, that they were big supporters, and saw nothing wrong with the sale of semi and automatic rifles. Kids were being gunned down at school and pop and grandma were all in favour of being surrounded by lethal weapons, one line of argument being that such armaments were needed for self-preservation. A gun begets a gun. I realised I was not going to get much joy on this topic and figured only the Amish could make any sense on this one.

We stopped shortly after leaving Los Angeles, and surprise surprise, I was back in Fullerton, the station where the taxi driver had dropped me to take a train to San Diego. At the time I figured he had made a mistake and didn't want to go into the city. Arriving at Fullerton the first time I thought I was in the middle of nowhere, and that it saw one train a day if it was lucky. But clearly, I was wrong, because here we were, first stop out of 31. No one got on or off, but what the hell, clearly the folks at Amtrak knew something about Fullerton that no one else did.

We pushed on, but night was rushing towards us, and I didn't hang around in the dining car for too long.

I was bushed. It had been a long day, and I was relieved to settle down in my bunk and fall into a peaceful sleep to the gentle rocking of the train, with the thoughts of a beautiful Cinderella being my last of the day.

Day 44 Amtrak

"In which various incidents will be recounted that could only have occurred on a railroad in America." - Jules Verne

"A train will bring you back to the place you came from, but it will not bring you home." - Jedediah Berry

On the rails again, chugging across America, heading east. Heading home. Home seemed like a distant place geographically and psychologically. I had been travelling two months and had rarely-thought of home. Sometimes, I wasn't even sure where home was. My son lived in Australia, my daughter in England, and me? I was drifting in a no-mans-land all of my own.

As Jules Verne had written of Phileas Fogg's sleeping arrangements on a similar train, *"The sheets were white and the pillows soft"*. Sleeping on trains was becoming a habit, and one I may consider for the future. I had never slept on one before trying to emulate Phileas, but here I was sleeping on them in Europe, Russia, China and now America.

I'm not such a good sleeper, and last night was no exception, but although I tossed and turned and was a little cold, I felt calm and happy and excited at the prospect of the train ride through America today. I would ask for another blanket for tonight!

Breakfast was taken with a new group of fellow travellers. The routine of joining two or three others was becoming normal. I liked the idea of never knowing who I would be joining. Meeting Americans who were either too scared to fly, or who were moving from one obscure place to another. No one was travelling - certainly not around the world. Only one third of Americans has a valid passport, so it was a fair bet that most on board the *Southwest Chief* weren't amongst them.

There was a greater risk of getting shot in America than starving to death. In fact, the food, if I continued at this pace, would probably be the death of me. I tried to imagine living on this ride - a train version of *Groundhog Day* - waking each morning in my compartment, a little cold from the night before. Would the *ground-hogging* reset my body weight to the day before, because if it didn't, I would be obese within a few months. The meal portions were enormous. The train should be renamed the *Southwest Chef*! Where food is concerned, Americans do not do things by halves. After 48 hours on this *Santa Fe Express*, I would unravel all the good work I had done on the *Hanjin Athens* in losing some kilos!

For a large part, the train follows the route of the *Santa Fe Trail*. There's a movie of the same name starring Errol Flynn and Olivia De Havilland. That's a real oldie, and who else pops up in that cowboy romance? Only the future President, Ronald Reagan, playing General George Armstrong Custer. Really, someone actually wrote that script - if only they had known how things would turn out. A General one day, a President the next! If it hadn't been for the (missing) Iraqi WMD, another General, Colin Powell, may have followed in Ronnie's cowboy boot-steps all the way to *The White House*. Fine lines, and misplaced loyalties can shape destiny.

I was pioneering east, heading to *"Chicago, Chicago that toddling town"*. But first I still had the Midwest to cross. A couple of hours after a massive breakfast, a welcome 30-minute stop at Albuquerque to stretch my legs and make some room for the inevitable ginormous lunch to follow.

I had a small stay in Albuquerque once. There sure must be a lot of snakes slithering around these parts. I say this because someone I met on my previous visit told me he had four rifles and two guns. When I asked him why, he said, 'To kill all of the snakes,' although he was grinning as he answered me.

But I remember that it is also famous for a hot-air balloon festival every October. That's still on my *bucket list*. Up there in the sky, no engine, floating around. I had tried gliding and that was pretty special. Riding the thermals, just like Steve McQueen as *Thomas Crown*... no wonder Faye Dunaway was literally swept off her feet. He was a real cool dude, Steve McQueen. Imagine how America would be now if he had made it to The White House - him or Clint?

I wandered down the platform, basking in the sun and feeling like life was pretty good. No frozen platforms as in Siberia, and not a Belarusian soldier in sight. All too soon we were back on board and heading to Las Vegas. That's Las Vegas, New Mexico, nothing like its namesake in Nevada, America's 24-hour playground. I made a *boys'-trip* there once, and for some bizarre reason, we stayed six nights and slept on average two hours per night. Three nights are really enough! No further comment is possible, because as we all know, *What happens in Vegas stays in Vegas*!

In the afternoon we roll on into Colorado and the air thins - Trinidad is at nearly 2,000 metres. I could be back in Mexico City, gasping for breath. Passing through nature and a whole new America. Gone are the hobos on Venice Beach, to be replaced by buffalo, deer and wild ponies. I never cease to be amazed at the diversity of this country. Diversity of nature and of people, all fused together - one enormous melting pot that has no equal on the planet.

The Amtrak Metropolitan Lounge is a treat reserved for those in the *sleeper* section. It's an observation carriage and occupies the last carriage of the train, and has glass panels in the roof, and comfortable swivel chairs to lounge out in and enjoy the views along the way. Phileas had a similar carriage on his train from San Francisco to New York, and a restaurant, and bunks. So, in 140 years not much had changed. I looked through the rear door window (I wonder if Phileas had also?), and it throws me back to untold numbers of images looking out the back of a train. The track disappearing to point zero, with only the landscape holding its shape and colours. And as the sun sets what majesty as the yellows change to gold, the sky finally turns to darker shades of pink and it passes into night.

Russian train management would do well to ride the Amtrak, on the *Santa Fe Trail,* to see what small changes they could adopt to turn the usual into the spectacular.

Over dinner I'm quite subdued. My stomach is full to bursting, and I manage to squeeze in a salad, just to justify staying at the table to chat to my fellow guests. By now I already know how the conversation is likely to go - but I endure in the hope of something new. The new would come tomorrow with the Amish. For this evening it's another grandma and pop double-act, taking the slow train to their grandchildren in Princeton, Illinois. They thought the train would give them to chance to see America. At their ages they should have already seen it! But you're never too old to try something new, so full credit to them. They thought the dining car was wonderful! Didn't we all?

I picked up an extra blanket and settled down for the night - the dazzling dark pink sky still fresh in my memory.

Day 45 Amtrak and Chicago

In which the American legal system, and sentencing, proves to be disproportionate to the crime committed

"America will never be destroyed from the outside. If we falter and lose our freedoms, it will be because we destroyed ourselves." - Abraham Lincoln

The *Southwest Chief* had rolled on through Colorado into Kansas during the night, whilst I thankfully slept like a baby.

I breakfasted with some Amish. They were exactly as I imagined them to be. Warm and cold at the same time. They were open to discuss any subject, but conscious of not causing offence, I tried to steer clear of anything contentious. The truth is, I was biting my tongue because there was so much I wanted to ask about their way of life.

One, whose name I didn't catch, told me the story of an Amish elder who had cut off the beard of another elder and had been sentenced to 15 years in prison. This sounded completely far-fetched, so I made a point to check it out. I have recounted this story to many: all have refused to believe it. But a quick check on the internet will confirm - it is true. In the U.K. you would serve less time for murder. That must have been one real fancy beard, probably a lifetime's growth.

This journey was reaching its conclusion and with a few more states navigated, we arrived in Illinois and finally Chicago Union Station. It was mid-afternoon and while I had enjoyed the ride, the meals had proved to be a challenge. Not the food - that was great - but the company. So many of those I spoke with seemed to be living on a different planet. It would go too far to call some of them cranks, but I will, they were. Perhaps all the sensible people were flying around the States?

This may sound like a pile of donkey poo, but most of those supporting the right to bear arms were also highly religious. There was a lot of saying grace going on in the dining-car, and one of the gun-zealous grace sayers even tried to give me a bible when we said our farewells. I respectfully said I had to decline the thoughtful gift on the grounds that I was a Buddhist.

Travelling will turn up all sorts of people, and I had experienced my fair share of them thus far on this trip. And what a mixed bag of society they were proving to be. Now, having left the wild west behind I was going to spend a few days in a big city; the third largest in the U.S. and with only three million people. How could that be?

We had blown into the Windy City, and it was both windy and cold. After sleeping on ships and trains for most of my journey, it was time to splash out and enjoy a little luxury. I found a swanky *old school* hotel in the centre of town and checked in for a stay I had long been waiting for: Chicago, very close to the top of my list of cities I wanted to explore. First Berlin, then Mexico and now Chicago - this journey around the world was providing some additional benefits.

I knew very little about Chicago, but I did know it had *Cloud Gate*, by the Indian-born British artist Sir Anish Kapoor. I had seen other large artworks by him in Milan (not so good) and Sydney (very good), so I was eager to see what is widely considered his best work. There was the Sears Tower, now renamed Willis Tower, and, I was told, a very good art museum, The Art Institute of Chicago. A full day tourist trail would be followed tomorrow. But for tonight I planned to hit the town.

The truth was, I had no idea where to *hit*. On

reaching the street outside the hotel, I was shocked at how cold it was. Which was crazy, because Siberia had reached minus 30 degrees centigrade, and it was only minus seven or eight here, but it felt much colder. The wind blowing off Lake Michigan was really making itself felt. Clearly it was known as the Windy City for good reason. I was going from one extreme to another, from the warmth of Los Angeles to be frozen in Chicago. It's little wonder Greg and his homeless friends travelled across country to spend their winters on Venice Beach.

Venturing a few blocks, I found a district full of bars and chose a lively one to grab an early dinner. Why do Americans make the effort to go out to dinner and then stay at a place less than an hour? It was something that always confused and amused me. In the at least two plus hours I stayed in that bar, the table next to mine was occupied at least three times. Couples were seated, fed and on their way. On my other side were two attractive women, perhaps in their late thirties, and without blowing my own trumpet, clearly giving me the eye. An opening wasn't really needed to get chatting. Jane and Meg were a wild pair, down from Vancouver on a business trip, although I never got to know what kind of business. They were both smart, well-groomed and sassy. I fancied Meg, the shyer one. Jane had the gift of the gab and wouldn't stop talking or flirting. Let me say here and now, I am no Robert Redford. When younger, and in those days, I had hair, I was compared to Sting. These days, it's more like Phil Collins or Bruce Willis. On such occasions I consider both comparisons flattering. So, quite how I got myself into these, fast becoming regular, situations on my travels, I'm not sure. It must be my natural charm!

I had few beers with those girls, and they were a lot of fun. Most of what was said has passed me by. I think

I tried to impress them with the story of my journey. What was clear was that Jane wasn't going to let her grappling hook go for me to hit on Meg. Ten years earlier, in fact maybe ten days earlier, I may have made more effort. But the truth is I'm getting older, and although that should not be any excuse, I was happy to just chat and have some fun. Perhaps my time in Mexico City was proving eventful enough for this week. I said my farewells to those crazy Canadians and headed back to my hotel, through the freezing Chicago night. Alone.

Day 46 Chicago Cloud Gate

In which not all clouds are found in the sky

"It's cloud illusions I recall. I really don't know clouds at all."
- Joni Mitchell

Today I would walk, and walk, and discover I really don't know clouds at all. The mean streets of Chicago were freezing, and me along with them. I thought I had left such temperatures behind in Siberia - but no, here I was again shivering as I made my way to Navy Pier on Lake Michigan. I stumbled upon a world city sign telling me London was 3,953 miles east and Shanghai 7,057 west. I was going full circle, and London was definitely getting closer.

The sun was shining, and the clear blue skies lifted my spirits, but not as much as the coffee and muffin I had for breakfast. American muffins are the best in the world, and that is an understatement. American cuisine is often highly criticised, but my experience over the years is to the contrary - sure, a lot of it is awful... processed meat... cheese from a squeezy bottle - but I've also eaten some amazing food, equal to anything in Paris or Milan.

Lake tours set off from the pier, but not many, if any, on a freezing winter's day, and I didn't have time for the lake. I was reaching into the clouds and getting all arty. I headed to Millennium Park, strolling back towards the city and the skyline was truly beautiful. Gleaming glass towers basking in the morning sunshine. Giants both old and new, more than a match for both Shanghai and London. I finally reached the park and the amazing spectacle of *Cloud Gate*. Locals call it *The Bean* - which is totally understandable, as it looks like a giant kidney bean. This single art piece has become Chicago's top tourist attraction and has come to be a symbol of the city, like the *London Eye*, which should only have been around for one year to celebrate the millennium, or Wall Street's *The Charging Bull*. How many movies has that bull appeared in?

The sun bounces off *Cloud Gate,* along with the distorted, reflected images of the many of us marvelling at this unique artwork. There are clouds floating across the sky all around me. I'm floating with them, filled with the joy of this day. A single piece of art making me feel so happy. I stay transfixed for over an hour. Part of the joy comes from watching people come and go in raptures at the sight before them. It sits above an ice-skating rink, which slowly fills with skaters. They really knew what they were doing when locating that shiny cloud. I eventually drag myself away, only to return later in the afternoon. The thing had me hooked, and when I think of Chicago, it's always *Cloud Gate* that comes to mind. I'm sure Sir Anish is very happy with himself!

The Chicago Art Institute is one of the best art galleries I have ever visited. Impressionist work abounds; the collection is a match for any gallery in the world. The range of art from the nineteenth and twentieth centuries is astounding. The Chagall *America Windows* would justify a visit on its own. I spend most of the rest of my day enthralled. I would have swapped two days in Shanghai for an afternoon with this art. Art is all the windows we need; it shows us the world.

In raptures and exhausted from the day's walking, I slowly returned to my hotel to crash for a few hours before heading out to dinner. A day to never forget, to add to the many memorable ones from my journey around the world, and a day so different from my previous 45.

I spent the evening at a local bar and thought about the wonders I had witnessed today. Yes, I have an interest in art, and I produce quite a bit of sculpture - so I'm biased, but I am always inspired by other artists' work. Their creative minds taking others to the places they alone have been able to visualise. The true greats inventing, and reinventing. Sometimes a mere few brushstrokes are enough to move us. This day had moved me, and it felt good. In a melancholy mood, I went to bed early, quickly falling into a deep sleep.

Day 47 Chicago Loopy

When shopping is always a good idea, even if you don't need anything

"I haven't been everywhere, but it's on my list." - Susan Sontag

Riding *The Loop*, my mind drifted back to the Pacific. I was now in a sea of people and mayhem, but back there I was in a sea of tranquillity. I was experiencing extremes, and all would leave their mark. I asked myself which mark would be the most permanent? I think even then I already knew.

I have had a love/hate relationship with America since first visiting in my early twenties. Such a grand and diverse country. The land of opportunity, but what had it become? I had first visited 30 years before. In many ways nothing had changed, and in others, so much. It's not for me to judge, but I believe it could have taken a different and better path. All those guns, all those unnecessary and tragic murders. The land of opportunity no more. But then in fairness, it was a country born out of bloodshed. Immigrants discovering the New World and all its riches. Natives nearly wiped out. A civil war, and what of today, what wars still raged?

Maybe I'm being too unkind. Maybe all countries are on the same path as the States. I think we notice more, we feel it more, because we hold the U.S. up as a beacon of light, with all that progression and hope, and if the light dims, it saddens all of us. A part of our light, our hope, dims with it.

The Loop is a famous part of the Chicago Metro system and has featured in countless movies. *The Loop* is nothing special, but it is above ground, suspended above the chaos, and thus affords great views of the city it serves. No one would speak of the *Circle Line* in London in the same way. It's a loop, but underground, it affords a view of nothing but other passengers and the litter-strewn floor of the world's oldest underground system.

Several *Batman* movies have filmed here - I thought Gotham City was in New Jersey? It's a very mixed-up world.

I had been here a couple of days now, and I was starting to get a feel for the place - *Home Alone*, was filmed here, little Kevin in the big, bad city. Didn't he know it's labelled the Murder Capital of America? Actually, the murder rate is high, but it's not the highest per capita. I remember staying in a hotel room in Times Square once that looked across to a counter that continually ticked over. That counter was registering the murders happening in the U.S. for that year. It ticked a lot during my short stay.

Why would anyone want to visit this crazy country? But we do, and we love it. My journeys across America had shown me the incredible diversity. Over the years I have travelled America horizontally and vertically and still there so much I have missed.

After a swanky brunch I headed to the shops intending to window shop - my bags were already full. But I ended up buying jeans, jackets, shirts and some smaller items. Everything is so cheap here, half the price of the U.K. and I, like everyone, cannot resist a bargain, even if it meant overloading my luggage. On a trip around Australia, I had set off with 20 kilos - when I checked in for my return flight, I had grown to 96 kilos. That was an expensive trip home - the excess baggage fee was higher than the airfare.

People often talk about Chicago being cold and windy and make no mistake - it is both. The daytime temperature was minus six degrees centigrade. The Windy City was living up to its name. Calamity Jane had, *blown in*, from Deadwood - my slow journey across country from Los Angeles to the metropolis had the same effect on my arrival. The vastness and urgency of the city left the peacefulness of my chugging train journey in its wake. People flocked to the big cities in search of riches, but what were they leaving behind? Probably, like Doris Day, they were leaving behind a little part of themselves.

Phileas took a train to Chicago to then catch another on his way to New York for his return to Europe. He never had time to enjoy this wonderful city. If fact on his entire journey, he never found the time to see much at all. He dashed around the world, eager to win his bet, and prove his buddies in the Reform Club wrong. His loss.

Travel Tip: When visiting the U.S., take empty bags.

Day 48 Chicago to Gallipolis

Where Phil, for the first time, takes to the road and experiences the freedom it offers

"Our battered suitcases were piled on the sidewalk again; we had longer ways to go. But no matter, the road is life." - Jack Kerouac - *On the Road*

It was time to blow out of this Windy City and head for the coast. Destination, Wilmington, North Carolina, from where I would take another container ship back to Europe. From this point, completing my journey in 70 days looked like a breeze. A different kind of *breeze* was to play its part halfway across the Atlantic.

So far, I had taken a great number of trains, the odd taxi and bus, and not forgetting one very long boat ride. The time had come to emulate Jack Kerouac and get *On The Road*. He crossed coast to coast. This was my second crossing, having previously made Los Angeles to Miami a few years earlier with my brother, Dave, and our sons. That journey could be another book… so much happened.

I opted for a hire car - pick-up Chicago and drop-off Wilmington - there was a premium to pay for that pleasure, although surprisingly low. I checked out of my city hotel home and headed down to the car hire office. The desk clerk enquired why I was headed out to the Carolinas. I tried to explain my journey, and was met, and not for the first time, by complete miscomprehension of what I was doing. He asked, 'Why don't ya fly, man?' Really, what could I say? Crossing State-lines for some Americans was like flying inter-continental. A soldier I would meet in Wilmington told me he had only left his homeland to serve in Iraq and had no plans to leave home again. That must have given him a very skewed view of the world outside the U.S. - Iraq and back!

I had come to learn over numerous visits to the U.S. that it is not a country, more a continent, and each state is a different country, as different as Sweden is to Portugal in Europe. In Texas I could buy a gun, but not in New Jersey. In Texas I could face the death penalty using that gun for murder, in New Jersey not. That Second Amendment of the U.S. Constitution reared its ugly head a number of times throughout my journey. Discussion on the point brought out very strong positions and emotions. Overall, I would say, from my unscientific poll, that 75% of Americans wanted to retain the right to bear arms. No wonder its removal was never mentioned come election time.

I was on the road, and it felt good to be behind the wheel of a car again, and to be heading into the wide-open spaces of America. Jack really did know what he was all about.

I left the city of Chicago with the early morning sun glittering off its skyscrapers in the rear-view mirror. I'd enjoyed my time in the Murder Capital and was relieved to have left unscathed. I'm not really a squeamish sort but those big cities of America, whilst on the one side fill me with joy, on the other side fill me with dread. Maybe that's part of the fascination, part of the buzz. I do not know another country in the world with such amazing diversity. You just don't know what to expect sometimes.

Driving in the U.S. is unique in my experience. Multi-lane carriageways with relatively slow-moving traffic. The other drivers always seem so respectful. I exclude city driving from this comment - no drive-by shooting on the quiet roads out of Illinois. It's a breeze at 55 or

60 miles per hour, cruise control and radio on, sun top down if you're lucky. It's a great way to travel. No wonder some Americans will drive an hour for a 45-minute dinner!

Crossing state lines has its risks. The speed limit can change, and the local law enforcement know the hotspots where an easy ticket can be handed out. My brother got caught out, and when stopped and asked if there were any firearms in the vehicle, made the fatal mistake of laughing as he replied, 'No.' That laugh had us all hauled off to the nearest, although it took 40 minutes to drive there, courthouse. Clearly that traffic cop was one of those without a passport, without a sense of humour, or perhaps he was just having a bad day. Didn't he know that only soldiers carry guns in the U.K.? I mean, even our cops don't have them!

Illinois quickly passed into Indiana, and as the morning drifted into a sunny afternoon, I moved into Ohio. When I considered driving, I wasn't sure how long it would take. I had a few spare days so didn't plan any night driving. I was just enjoying the feeling of the open road with the radio blaring away. I was in a good mood; the trip was going well. I was making good progress, and life just felt... good. Some days are like that, you can't really explain why you feel as you do, you just do. And the opposite is of course true, when you're down, you're down.

Around 6 p.m. I started to flag. Time to call it a day. I was in southeast Ohio and stopped outside the town of Gallipolis. Basically, I was in the middle of nowhere in the middle of America, but it didn't concern me. I needed a shower, some food and a bed. I pulled off the highway onto a slip road and into the nearest motel. A motel, like any one of the many throughout America. Motels seemed to be unique to this country. Where else did you find them in such quantities. It was all about the road, being on the road, or at least it used to be. Moving first with horse-drawn wagon-carts then trains and then automobiles. Cheap flights had probably wiped out some of the motel population. But thankfully many survive, and a few thrive. I had chosen a survivor. Gallipolis was never going to attract a crowd. As the waitress told me later, 'People can't wait to get away from this place.' I think she was one of them, I certainly was - I wanted away from this place as soon as I was refreshed. The road stretched ahead of me to the coast, and the sea was calling me.

Travel Tip: The option to make a one-way trip in a hire car proved to be a good one. The surcharge was relatively low, especially considering the benefits.

Day 49 Gallipolis to Beaufort

In which another ocean is reached with time to kill

"Hello. I'm Forrest. Forrest Gump."

I hit the road early, life felt good, and I was enjoying the freedom of being on the road with a destination in mind, but no urgency to reach it.

America was built to drive. Great highways, slow speeds that take the stress out of the ride. The radio playing middle of the road music, and me singing with joy. In *Broken Flowers*, Bill Murray is on the road, on a mission, an ageing *Don Juan* crossing the country tracking down his former lovers. I'm not sure whether to take it as a compliment or not, but when I mentioned my writing the story of this journey to Sofia, my Trans-Siberian travel companion, she said I should call it *"Around the World with 65 women"*. I'm certainly no *Don Juan*, but as I drove, the movie did rear its head, along with so many others, like *Rain Man* and *Planes, Trains & Automobiles*. There are too many to mention. America is one long road movie.

I hadn't slept well - so much buzzing through my mind. The only solution was to grab an early breakfast and get moving.

There are moments in life - not days, but moments - which lodge, for no apparent reason, and get stuck there. I was crossing West Virginia, and John Denver's *Take Me Home, Country Roads* played on the radio. It almost made me cry. The same happened a couple of years later, when, arriving at the car park of *Graceland* with my two kids on our *American Music Tour*, I went to cut the ignition just as *Walking in Memphis* started to play; we sat in silence and listened, and then all marvelled at the coincidence. It stayed with me, always will, and I always think about that car park when I hear any Elvis song. Just like I think of that moment on the road in West Virginia. *"Country roads, take me home, to the place I belong"* - and they sure were - I was heading east, and heading home.

The snow-laden mountains of the Virginias were a sight to see, and never be forgotten. America, the land of such amazing diversity in all aspects. The geography, the people; a continent forged together as a single nation. I have yet to visit a country in the world with such multiplicity. A country I never left, without knowing I would return.

There was virtually no traffic on the road. Winter roads on a rarely used route, but the highways were still top class, and the lack of company gave me time to cruise and think. Memories flooded my mind - the recent Amtrak ride, Venice Beach and Cinderella, and inevitably the Pacific. Always the Pacific - it's top of the memory list from my circumnavigation, and always will be. Something lodged in my mind and doesn't leave. Day 30 and the catharsis, me a changed man, not consciously at that moment, but later as my response to the experience of my journey around the world took shape.

States came and went, Ohio, West Virginia, Virginia and eventually into North Carolina. It felt as if I was a passenger and not the driver. The car just seemed to roll on, oblivious of my presence.

I stopped early afternoon for lunch and studied a map and decided that, with time on my hands, I would not go directly to Wilmington, from where I would set off across the Atlantic. I decided to stay up the coast for a night. My new destination was Beaufort. I had no idea why I chose Beaufort, North Carolina, but when I arrived and later researched the place, I realised why it was considered *America's Coolest Small Town*. Totally charming. And the backdrop of some of my favourite movies. Forrest Gump had been here. *The Big Chill* was set here, would it end? When was I going to move here? Port Townsend in Washington State finally had a competitor.

And let me stress the location as North Carolina, because South Carolina also has a Beaufort. More research revealed it was as an equally cool place. Was a vacation to compare the two Beauforts on the cards? Not on this trip, but it seemed like a nice idea.

As I parked the car, I noticed Abraham Lincoln was on the number plate. It was an Illinois plate, but he was born in Kentucky. Clearly, he was in demand, every U.S. State wanted their slice. Illinois, the *Land of Lincoln*. Kentucky would have something to say about that!

I found a waterside hotel and settled in for a great stay. Water everywhere - the town is almost surrounded by it. Beaufort consists of 68 islands, and as much water as land at high tide. It had a French and British feel about the place - this I noticed as soon as I started walking around. The same had struck me on arrival in Akaroa on New Zealand's South Island. The only difference was Akaroa had been French, whereas Beaufort was founded and settled by my countrymen and named after the Duke of Beaufort. Us Brits soon grabbed Akaroa away from the French, but the legacy of good cafes and pastries still remain there.

Beaufort oozed the kind of old-English charm that made you want to relocate. Wooden jetties and waterside shacks in abundance, and as I discovered later that evening, seafood to die for. I hadn't intended to relive my time in Akaroa or Port Townsend, but something had drawn me to Beaufort, and I was grateful to relive similar wonderful memories in this endearing place.

Totally unintentional on my part, but I had set foot in Beaufort and Santa Monica within a week. Tom as Forrest had taken longer and preceded me in crossing America from Santa Monica to Beaufort. In the movie we see him running for seven minutes of screen time - I had covered the journey in seven days. *"That's all I have to say about that."*

Day 50 Beaufort to Wilmington

In which if playing dumb is what is required, then playing dumb it is

"You can't arrest me, I'm a rockstar" – Sid Vicious

'Put your hands up, and get out of the vehicle.' This said by one of the three soldiers pointing their rifles at me. Following a morning of bliss, I had got myself into a right pickle.

I had found a gem, and it shined bright and colourful this sunny morning as I made my way over Beaufort Bridge. That bridge is gone now, replaced. They call it progress! I'm glad Forrest and I crossed the old bridge, something we have in common, and which is no longer possible.

I was moving on to Wilmington, and my destiny with another container ship - the *MV Independent Voyager* would be taking me to Europe in three days' time. Well, that's what I thought. A raging Atlantic would have something to say about that!

I was a little sad to leave the unexpected gem that was Beaufort. It was a relatively short drive to Wilmington, so I opted for the beach route down the 21-mile length of Bogue Banks. What a treat. The sun was shining on endless beaches stretching the entire length of the island. Although it was winter, the hidden treasure of towns and villages gave a window on what could be expected during the summer months, when tens of thousands of tourists would descend on this slice of Atlantic heaven. The lucky ones would own or rent a wood-clad house with beach access.

Before making this trip, I had given very little thought to the Carolinas. I only had impressions from movies like *Message in a Bottle*, and *The Notebook*, two of my favourite love stories. I do have a romantic side, even if it's well hidden! Like Beaufort before it, what I saw made me want to return for a longer stay, and during warmer months. I stopped for a coffee and thought about making a future trip down the east coast from Maine to Miami - spring into summer. Perhaps the reverse, Miami in spring into Maine in summer. Either way it struck me as a great idea. To be made with female company perhaps. Just to add to the romanticism.

Just when you think you've seen all there is to see of a country, something pops up to surprise you. The old saying that the world is getting smaller just is not true. It's just that we have the chance to see more, and in so doing, discover there is so much more than we thought.

The names alone made me want to return - Atlantic Beach, Indian Beach, Emerald Isle. It was hard to imagine too much concern about gun control in this paradise.

Morning passed to afternoon, and I headed on to Wilmington. I saw there were some back roads that might take a little longer but offered the chance of avoiding the highway. I had been enticed by my drive down the Atlantic. And herein lay my downfall.

Unbeknown to me I had somehow driven straight onto a back route into the Marine Corps base, Camp Lejeune. I started to acquire an uneasy feeling when I noted there were no other cars on the road, but I pushed on. I passed an apparently empty wooden hut. Only a fortunate glance in the rear-view mirror told me someone was inside. I made a U-turn to go back and ask the way. This was when I met three new friends.

The boys back in Belarus had been quiet, and although stern-faced, had presented no threat. None had pointed a rifle at me or shouted at me. The Marine

Corps is reserved for serious soldiering, those guys don't mess around. Bizarrely I felt incredibly calm. Was I becoming impervious to such situations? The rifles should have spooked me, but they didn't.

I got out of the car, arms up. I didn't even feel nervous; what was happening to me? Suddenly I was getting used to landing myself in crazy situations. I decided to get in first. 'I'm lost,' I said. It really was feeble, even if honest. They looked confused and then bemused. An English accent for sure worked in my favour. They lowered their weapons and came closer. No, I didn't know I had entered a military establishment - well I didn't until I made the U-turn. Yes, I could guess it was against the law. And very yes, I really was lost and was trying to reach Wilmington. I decided not to mention my mission, or the fact that in the past couple of months I had visited both sworn enemies in Russia and China. Good sense told me to keep stum on those golden nuggets. I prayed they wouldn't want to see my passport. It was brand new with only a few classic stamps inside. The best of all being the entry cancelled in Belarus.

First Belarus and now America - whatever next? I thought I had left all this malarky behind in Europe. I was closing in on the home stretch and really didn't need this kind of hassle.

I was politely directed back the way I had come and told to be more careful next time - they also suggested I buy a map. I would say I got off lightly, after-all I had actually got past the guard post. Again, I was being turned back, but fortunately this detour would not prove as problematic as that through Poland.

Arriving in Wilmington late afternoon, I cruised around a little and opted for a grand modern hotel overlooking the river. With easy access to the downtown district and waterfront, it was a perfect place to base myself for three nights of comfort before my Atlantic crossing. After negotiating a good deal, I found myself in the most luxurious surrounding of my entire stay. The room would pass for a small apartment in London and had far reaching views over the water to countryside in the distance.

I took a stroll along the riverbank and made my way into a district like that of San Diego's Gaslamp. There were several good-looking bars and restaurants to choose from. Three nights here would be easy to fill. My luck was to select the one with the best nachos I had ever eaten. Those tasty morsels and a few beers had me set for the night. I decided on an early one, even though I met a few interesting people. I promised to, and did, return the following night.

Day 51 Wilmington

In which a trip down the coast results in a serious intake of calories

"But the English gentleman asked nothing. He was not travelling; he was tracing a circle. He was matter in orbit around the globe, following the laws of physics." - Jules Verne

Sand between my toes and the cool Atlantic around my ankles. The sun shines through the broken clouds and warms my back. The beaches south of Wilmington are as welcoming as their northern brethren.

I decided to explore further afield and headed down the coast and out onto the peninsula with the Cape Fear River on the western side - Fort Fisher as my final destination. *Cape Fear...* just the name spoke of horror and disaster. And it had its fair share of both. Robert De Niro had broken his teeth to play the ever threatening Max Cady, he was still in his *method* acting mode back then. I made a point to see the movie again upon my return to London.

Carolina Beach, Wilmington Beach and on to Kure, where I strolled the beach and ambled around the pier for an hour. Finally, I found a beachfront restaurant and stopped for a massive lunch. I needed the energy, so my diet was pushed to one side for a couple of days before hitting the Atlantic. Who knew what might be served on board the *Independent Voyager*? Filled with fish, shrimp, salad and fries and the largest cheesecake I've ever eaten, I moved on to the Fort Fisher State Historic Site, which has remains from the American Civil War.

The drive was a joy; sun shining all the way and temperatures warm enough for shirtsleeves, the golden sands leading down to a calm Atlantic with mild surf rippling the beach. This was the lull before the storm as the roiling Atlantic would grow to storm-force and play her part in delaying my arrival home. But for now, the calm waters were inviting and filling me with good vibes.

Fort Fisher was an interesting place, both in and out of the museum. As I mooched around, I was taken back to that devastating pointless war. Phileas had missed it by only a few years - he had stayed north of all the action, making his Atlantic crossing from New York. Fort Fisher was a strategic place - it finally fell to the Union, but the cost in lives was enormous. Americans killing Americans (much like today), with the civil war claiming more than ten times the number lost in Vietnam (and the least we say about that war the better). It remains America's most deadly war. When I think about America today with its multitude of racial issues and social disharmony, I wonder what greater mess the place would be in, had the Confederates won.

Safe Haven was one of the movies filmed in and around Fort Fisher. Breezing around the place and over to the ferry terminal and castle, I could really see all those wonderful locations. Multi-coloured wood-clap houses, wooden jetties and thousands of sailing and fishing boats. A perfect location for any movie. Bobby De Niro must have loved the seafood whilst scaring the life out of the locals.

Wilmington is also nicknamed Wilmywood. A testament to the many movies filmed in the city and surrounding area. Wilmywood. Original!

I'm still exercising every day, somehow maintaining the regime I started on the *Hanjin Athens*. Judging by my clothing, it's actually working. Dieting is not really my thing; I enjoy my food too much. And exercising is not my thing, so I fully expect to return to my normal weight within a few weeks of returning home - but for now I was stuffing my face with goodies, and it felt great.

The Atlantic coastline stretches further than the eye can see, its sandy beaches must be teeming with holidaymakers in the summer. But right now, there was hardly anyone around, and I was loving the space. I headed back up to Wilmington and stopped a few times to take in the views and grab a coffee. Italians may turn up their noses, but I'm a lover of American coffee - probably because I don't think of it as *real* coffee - but a likeable alternative!

Reaching Wilmington, I crashed in my room for a few hours. Eventually, I roused myself to slip out for a couple of beers at one of the many fine bars lining North Front Street in the historic district of the city. The folks of Wilmington were mighty friendly - in any bar I entered I would find happy customers waiting to have a chat. I guess there were not too many out-of-towners around in February - August would be a completely different kettle of fish.

Day 52 Wilmington Cake Lunch

Where Phil gets lost but a good Samaritan points him in the right direction

"Let's face it, a nice creamy chocolate cake does a lot for a lot of people; it does for me." — Audrey Hepburn

After dropping off the hire car, it was a long walk back into town. Longer than I thought but I had time to kill. Melancholy had set in - was it the prospect of the upcoming voyage? Days alone at sea, me, myself and I, and thoughts of home? I wasn't really sure, and neither of where I was headed, I just set off in the direction I had driven, back towards the city centre. An hour or so later I realised I was lost. At some point I started paying attention to my surroundings and deduced I was in a ghetto area. Escape, but how? J.R.R. Tolkien said, *"Not all those who wander are lost,"* but I was, and well and truly!

I found a youth centre, and went inside, finally finding a kindly elderly woman, who raised her eyebrows and asked what I was doing in 'this part of town?' Good question really, and I wish I knew. 'I'm lost,' I lamely answered, to which she shot back with a smile, 'You sure are.' She escorted me outside and pointed me in the direction of the quickest route to where I should be. She asked if she should call a cab for me - which sounded ominous - it wasn't even midday! I walked. Fast. Walking west and feeling safer as I passed each new block, and finally emerging into the historic district and familiar territory. I hadn't really felt threatened in any way, but the cab remark had spooked me a little.

There was only one thing to do. Eat, and eat sweet. On reaching the Riverwalk, I headed straight to a tearoom I had previously walked past. Therein, lunch became a pot of Earl Grey tea and two enormous cakes. One a kind of Victoria sponge covered in cream and strawberries, the other the largest brownie I had ever seen. Americans simply don't do food by halves. I savoured every mouthful. Diet blown, there was always the Atlantic on which I could try and redeem my bad behaviour. On a sugar high and with a map in hand I went on what is locally called the *Gallery Tour*. Wilmington is no Chicago, and the local galleries are not the Chicago Art Institute, however art is art and the local artists had given it their best shot.

Day 53 Wilmington Stuck

In which as Shakespeare said, *"Nothing comes from doing nothing."* So Phil did something

"When nothing goes right... go left" - Slogan on my T-Shirt

I was done with Wilmington and was supposed to be setting sail. The gods and storms were conspiring against me. But curling up in a ball and moaning wasn't going to get me anywhere.

Setbacks had been in short supply recently, so this one could be handled in my stride. There was no point doing nothing when there is always something to do. So, I looked for parts of Wilmington I had not yet seen.

In the morning I took a taxi to the container terminal, and immediately knew something was amiss, and something was missing. And that something was a very large container ship. I found the port agent who informed me that the *MV Independent Voyager* would only arrive in the early hours of the following morning, as she had encountered severe storms on her crossing to Wilmington. Ominous. I was told to return the following morning.

I was stuck in Wilmington, a small city I thought I had exhausted in my three days there.

I took a taxi back into town and quickly found a motel. I checked-in, dumped my things and scanned the tourist leaflets for something to fill my day. I settled for a tour of one of Wilmington's oldest houses. Really? Was I scraping the barrel? I exchanged the sea for the river, and booked a Cape Fear River tour, which took in a glimpse of the battleship *USS North Carolina*, which was moored across from the Riverwalk.

But first, brunch, and frustration led me to a diner, which was clearly in competition with the tea shop in trying to over-fill its clients. I left, stuffed, and walked to Bellamy House. Old in America is relative. Bellamy House was a beautiful, mostly wood-constructed building. Although it's a house with an identity crisis, part antebellum (I have no knowledge of Latin, but read that it means *before* the *war,* in this case only just), part Greek, and part Italian architecture. I joined a tour which made me feel like a teenager again. My fellow tour-mates were all well into their retirement. They were waxing lyrical about the age of the building. I wanted to scream 'Come on, folks!' It was built in 1861, the year the American Civil War kicked-off. A year after this journey around the world I moved into a house in Gloucestershire, England built in 1412; that was old, and it had a ghost!

I moved on from Bellamy House and a short walk brought me to the Riverwalk, and boarding point for an aquatic view of the Cape Fear River and surroundings. I should have been heading into the Atlantic, and here I was cruising along a river. But I would be back on this river tomorrow, further downstream, and that time being piloted into the Atlantic beyond. My grey-haired *house-tour-mates* had become my *shipmates*, as, unbeknown to me, they had tagged along behind me. It looked like we were on the same day-tour! The *USS North Carolina* was hiding in full view down a creek just off the river. At 222 metres she was close to the length of the *Independent Voyager*. She was getting on a bit now, having been launched in 1940. After a short career of only 22 years, she was made into a museum in 1962, and has been sitting in that creek ever since.

I felt I had been sitting in Wilmington even longer. I was eager to get on my way, get onboard the *Independent*

Voyager set off across my second ocean.

A day that started with disappointment turned out to have some nice surprises. Nothing ventured, nothing gained. My time in North Carolina was rounded off with some classic tourist sights, and I would leave the city, once known as New London, feeling I had seen just about all there was to see. New London indeed! I would soon be heading to the one and only, London, England. Homeward bound, with only The Pond to cross.

Day 54 Wilmington MV Independent Voyager

In which the sea beckons, and at a second attempt, the ship casts off to Europe

"The sea, once it casts its spell, holds one in its net of wonder forever." - Jacques Yves Cousteau

Yesterday had been a massive disappointment. I arrived at the port to find my passage back to Europe not there. Like Phileas Fogg in Hong Kong, showing up at the port to find his ship to America already departed the previous evening. My hope was that it would show up today. Heavy storms delayed the vessel mid-ocean. That didn't sound good. Where was the peace of the Pacific? The Atlantic threatened to be a whole different *ballgame*. And so it proved to be in the days that followed.

Déjà vu… I was in a taxi heading to the port… again. I was filled with apprehension, and uncertain if I would find my passage back to Europe arrived yet.

Finally, the ship's name came into view, and with a huge sigh of relief, I had my first glimpse of home for the next ten or so days, The *MV Independent Voyager*. I saw orange containers being off-loaded from the blue holds and deck of a ship which was clearly smaller than the *Hanjin Athens*. Why had she been delayed so long? What wild seas lay ahead? Questions flooded my mind. A touch of the Trans-Siberian nervousness entered for the first time in a long time. Was *she* a she? My pub-quiz knowledge told me all ships were *shes*, but the two I'd sailed on didn't sound very feminine.

On closer inspection she was definitely smaller. The bridge was a six-floor apartment block located at the back, stern. Containers stretched out in front of it, right up to the prow. I wouldn't be exercising so extensively on this voyage. As fate and the Atlantic would dictate, hardly at all, in fact.

But I was very excited. I mean, by now I was an experienced sailor. I had crossed the Pacific, I was an *old hand,* I would buy a pet parrot on my return to Blighty. Sailing, a bit like trains, was a new experience for me. I was invited on a three-day mini-cruise to Belgium once. Other than the endless good food and casino, not much had appealed to me about being *onboard.* Here I was about to embark on another significant voyage, and for sure, there was no casino or any other entertainment. But I was getting used to life at sea, so I knew I would find a rhythm, find a way to pass the long days in the inevitable solitude that awaited me. I remember feeling some relish at the prospect. A lasting feeling that the Pacific changed me forever has never faded. At the time, as I waited to board, I wondered if the Atlantic would have the same impact.

My first impression had been correct, this was a smaller ship. All the cabins and various rooms were housed in the *apartment block*, including my much smaller cabin. The *Hanjin Athens* cabin was two or three stars, this was definitely one star, with barely room to swing a cat. Definitely not the height of luxury, and on reflection, a theme for my entire journey. From the trains of Europe and Siberia to the ocean crossings, I had found very little in the way of luxury. Basic would best sum up my Phileas' accommodation, which was probably equal to what Phileas had encountered. This cabin had no carpet, which added to the basicness for the next 10 days. But I would not let a missing carpet impact my exercise routine. I had lost some weight on my journey, and I intended to keep it lost.

I was met by the first officer, Alex, a Serbian, and as it turned out all the officers were the same nationality.

Germans before, now Serbs. The common thread was the crew - on both ships being Filipinos, who outnumbered the officers three to one.

Alex was pleasant - one of those people who went through life with a permanent smile on his face. Perhaps 40, and like many of the officers I met, with a family back home waiting for his four-month tour of duty to end. It really was a strange life for those sailors! They were usually home for a couple of months before embarking on another tour. I figured they worked nine out of 12 months on average. No one seemed in a rush to change jobs and become landlubbers. In fact, at least with the officers, they were on the look-out for progression and promotion, which inevitably meant more money.

He gave me a brief tour of the ship, which involved a lot of stairs. There were no elevators and all the doors had double handle systems. The *Independent Voyager* had clearly been designed for the transatlantic route. When asked about the delay in the crossing over, Alex said, 'Rough,' and the journey to Antwerp, 'Rough.' Rough... no poodle parlour ride home this! When pushed on a possible arrival date, he guessed at March fifth. Still on schedule. I was cheered that although later then I initially thought, I would at least make it. Three days later, as I lay on the floor of my cabin, having been thrown out of my bunk in a storm close to where the Titanic sank, I wasn't so confident.

I settled into my claustrophobic cabin without a feeling of joy. Clearly, trips out to the deck and some circuits would be necessary. But the storms we encountered, one after another, would have a say on that.

After studying some graphics I found in a stairwell, I realised the ship was new, being built in 2011 and was half the dead weight size of the *Hanjin Athens*. It had a newish feel about it, which didn't explain why an elevator had not been installed. Maybe the threat of storms across the Atlantic had something to do with that.

At dinner, I met the other officers. Very welcoming people, and very engaging. On the *Hanjin Athens*, I had to sit alone for my meals. 'This is your table, Mr Hill,' the German captain had made clear at my first meal. No such formality with the Serbs, I sat with the captain, Zorin, and other officers. Zorin was a handsome man, also 40-something. He put me at ease immediately, and at almost every meal, we spoke about football. They were all football crazy, those Serbs. A common language, from Manchester United to Real Madrid, Pele to Maradona, mealtimes were a very welcome relief from the solitude of dining on the Pacific, as was the open invitation to visit and stay on the bridge as often as I liked. That was an offer I frequently took up and was one of the only escapes from my cabin.

I never found out if Zorin was a Christian name or surname. I'm not sure why I never asked him. Maybe out of respect for the fact he was the captain, probably just because it didn't really matter. A James Bond baddie was called Zorin, played by Christopher Walken. But Captain Zorin wasn't a baddie, and he was certainly no James Bond either. Just one of life's *happy people.*

I spent the evening on the bridge, watching the orange boxes stacking up. The containers were evenly placed across the length and breadth of the ship. Unfortunately, high enough to completely block any view from my one-star, soon to be reduced to half-star, cabin. Around 8 p.m. a U.S. ship's pilot boarded, following completion of loading, to navigate us out of the Cape Fear River towards the open seas. We passed

Fort Fisher, which I had visited three days earlier. Wilmington is quite a way up that river. The battles that had raged proved a turning point in the American Civil War. The unionists had eventually captured Wilmington, the last major port of the Confederates on the Atlantic coast. Like the deserting Confederates, I was now deserting the city and U.S. and like many of those soldiers, I was heading home.

I was on the bridge when the pilot left the ship and Zorin and his officers took us into the Atlantic. I had the realisation that this last major leg of my journey was bringing my adventure to an end, and it was not really a pleasant feeling. I felt a mixture of emotions. The *boat ride* itself wasn't disturbing me, it was something else. Something akin to watching a good movie coming to an end. I wanted it to go on, at least for a little while longer. And although I still had to make this crossing, I could see the light at the end of the tunnel already, and I realised I was quite enjoying being in the dark!

Day 55 Atlantic Storms

In which Phil is restricted to life inside the ship and adjusts his routine accordingly

"Writing fiction, especially a long work of fiction, can be a difficult, lonely job; it's like crossing the Atlantic Ocean in a bathtub. There's plenty of opportunity for self-doubt." - Stephen King

Alex was right, rough. I slept badly and the Atlantic was already making itself felt. As the day progressed, the weather became stormier, and storms continued to escalate throughout most of the voyage.

We set off a day later than scheduled and would be delayed a further day. My expected 63 days was becoming 65.

I started to think about following a regime. Wandering the decks was clearly going to prove difficult under the stormy conditions and Zorin told me to expect very little time outside. That left me going between my small cabin, a room they called the gym, which had one functioning piece of equipment - a cross-trainer - and the bridge. At least I was made very welcome on the bridge, and throughout the trip it would afford me spectacular views forward over the prow and Atlantic beyond.

Yet despite the cramped conditions, my first impressions were very positive, especially regarding the officers. They were all friendly and engaging. Every meal was spent at one communal table, and they were curious and interested in my journey and life. And they were more than willing to speak of themselves and their adventures at sea and in port! This was a massive step-up from the cold isolation of dining across the Pacific.

Being friendly to people costs nothing and, unlike them, I was new to this game. I had found some sea-legs but was still wearing shorts. The distance my shipmates on the *Hanjin Athens* kept has always disturbed me. Given the choice to repeat one of these two sea voyages, I would opt for the Atlantic and its friendly Serbs, even if I was restricted to staying inside.

I don't want to be critical of the officers on the *Hanjin Athens*, I just think they were a reflection of their leader. Any team captain will set the tone for the team; Zorin's was friendly and open and his team followed suit.

The ship itself was very new. You could still smell the fresh paint, like sitting in a new car - even after a month or two, the newness remains. I was surprised that, as new as it was, there were very limited facilities for the crew to enjoy. The dayroom was quite small, and I think I only used it once. The gym was tiny and not well equipped. There was, however, a good video collection, so the coming ten days would be filled with movies.

My routine became breakfast, exercise, reading, lunch, exercise, movie, dinner, movie. All this interspersed with regular visits to the bridge. The resulting effect was that I had much more time with my shipmates.

The Atlantic was a ferocious place. We would crash through the waves and the spray would be flung from the prow over a hundred metres back to smash onto the bridge windows. The wipers were on overtime.

The food was an upgrade also. Mostly buffet style, instead of table service. More than anyone would eat. It reminded me of those hotel buffets I used to enjoy, and later regret, during my working years. If it feels like it's free, I'll eat it! A bit like plane food. How often do people eat in the terminal, and then still find room for the cardboard sandwich served on board?

The weather worsened as night descended on the *Independent Voyager*, and as I took one final visit to the bridge before calling it a night, I was being thrown around ascending the staircase and even more so once I reached the top. Holding on to something, anything, was essential. The deep blackness of night at sea left a strange feeling of blindly heading into the unknown. Had that not been true of my whole journey so far? I set off from London having no idea of what I was really getting myself into. The trip to Moscow was filled with drama; a drama I would not care to repeat. The train ride across Siberia had also presented its own challenges. Certainly not the glamorous experience I had anticipated. And now I was on my second ocean, and how different they were proving to be. A common theme of both being the feeling of isolation and floating with no control over my destiny. I couldn't just get off and take a different course. Once on board, you stayed on board until reaching port, and across those massive oceans, ports of call were in short supply.

So, I remained headed into the unknown, as I had been for 55 days. Trying to always head east, a compass point steering my passage around the world.

Day 56 Atlantic Espresso

Where a small machine brings big rewards

"I judge a restaurant by the bread and by the coffee." - Burt Lancaster

The smell was enough to make my mouth water. The smell was enough to prick my senses and my mind and carry me to faraway lands. To Milano, to The Great Ocean Road in Australia, to yesterday and to tomorrow.

Smells will do that. Our senses taking us to our past and bringing our history to the present. Today's history lesson was provoked by the espresso available 24/7 on the bridge. Another good reason for me to venture up to that storm-swept window with its truly unique view.

One of the Filipinos is a trainee officer, and he seemed to spend his entire day on lookout duty. What's he looking for? The radar would pick-up anything of a reasonable size: some passing yachtsman or fishing vessel. Well, he's looking for anything, literally. With the sea so rough, things get missed. So, he looks and I guess hopes not to see, because it strikes me that if he does see something, then we may have a problem. They found Tom Hanks drifting after escaping his *Cast Away* island. I always wondered, and more so today, how long it would take to stop and turn around the ship.

Sleep was proving a problem under the prevailing conditions. I only dropped off around 3 a.m., so felt somewhat drained. I hit the cross-trainer but had little enthusiasm or energy for it. I could strap my phone to it with elastic bands and watch movies as I exercise. That helped. Those last few kilos I was trying to lose were proving elusive. I'd try and make more effort tomorrow.

So, in compensation for the lack of exercise, I cut

back on the calories at lunch and dinner.

On the bridge, I took a look at the radar and general chart of the Atlantic. I notice something on the screen and ask Zorin what it is. To my surprise, he tells me, it marks where the *Titanic* sank. Poor Leo and Kate freezing in the icy waters. Looking at that raging sea, I'm amazed anyone survived, even in a lifeboat. Quite why modern sea charts show this is a mystery, and Zorin didn't know why that particular disaster should be highlighted all those years later. What's really weird is that she sank well south of our route to Europe. Again, we were sailing north to eventually turn east, just like on the Pacific. What on earth was that iceberg doing so far south? I guess we can blame it on global warming. I'm assured that the *Independent Voyager* has never got anywhere near an iceberg. So, we were northwest of the Titanic sinking, and I was mighty thankful for that because the weather chart shows a massive storm right over where X marked the spot. We were steering towards quieter waters, or at least I thought we were!

Day 57 Atlantic 7 Cylinders

When the smaller the engine does not necessarily mean the slower the speed

"Feeling sorry for yourself and your present condition is not only a waste of energy but the worst habit you could possibly have." - Dale Carnegie

I was in the engine room. Giant ear-splitting cylinders chugged away, and I was transported back to another engine room. That one on the Pacific. Was I stuck in another *Groundhog Day*? Surely not?

But first a breath of fresh air. Finally, I was allowed outside, but as I looked at what was a fairly low handrail and water-washed deck, I wasn't filled with confidence that strolling around would be as liberating as on the Pacific. In fact, I was escorted for 30 minutes by the chief officer, Perica, who like his fellow officers was very friendly. He told me to take care, and I really didn't need that advice. I appreciated that nervous half hour stroll and wasn't too disappointed when we went back inside. He told me the sea would be calmer tomorrow and I could go out on my own. I was looking forward to that; being outside gave me a connection to the sea that I didn't feel inside. The smell of salt, and wind and sea-spray on my face; like breathing fresh air again after scuba diving.

The afternoon visit around the engine room was conducted by Igor, who was in his early 50s, and who I mistakenly took for a Serb. He turned out to be Russian. He had a real sense of humour, and obvious affection for his beloved engines. Big boy's toys don't come much bigger. I commented on the fact that the engine appeared so much smaller than on the *Hanjin Athens*. For a brief second, I thought he took this remark as a slight on his babies. He quickly recovered though, but had no real comment on this. I thought it could be a different technology, but perhaps it was just connected to the vessel tonnage, and even route. As far as I could discern, the *Independent Voyager* stuck to trans-Atlantic crossings. It was definitely hitting the speeds of my Pacific crossing, and was perhaps even faster, despite the poor weather. We had time to make up!

One clear difference between the two engine-rooms was that Igor would not permit me to take any photographs. So maybe there was more to those smaller engines than meets the eye. Or perhaps it had something to do with Igor being Russian.

I asked about socialising, and he told me the only evening there was any kind of *get together* was on a Saturday, when the officers would meet in the Officers' Recreation Room. I made a note to not miss it. It turned out to be a lot of fun, and there was a fair amount of alcohol sloshing around. Captain Schmidt would certainly not have approved.

Day 58 Atlantic Walkie Talkie

Fun when it's least expected puts a smile on Phil's face

"I may not have gone where I intended to go, but I think I have ended up where I intended to be." - Douglas Adams

"Broadsword calling Danny Boy…" My brother is always quoting that line from *Where Eagles Dare* - Richard Burton's clipped voice trying to thwart the Germans. And it came back to me now as I stood feeling like a complete idiot. I tried again, 'Over and out,' no response. And again, 'Over and out.' This time without the walkie talkie, 'Can you hear me?' 'Yes,' came the reply, Igor was standing four metres away, so he had no reason not to hear me! We were on walkie talkie practice before he let me venture outside on my own.

What I didn't get was that if I slipped overboard the walkie talkie wouldn't be much help. I would be a goner.

The day started calmly, calm enough for me to be let off my lead and venture outside alone. But after lunch, the Atlantic did an about-turn and the seas roiled and boiled and life as I had known it these past few days returned to normal.

I had enjoyed the respite and my moment outside alone. Me alone with the Atlantic, but not for long enough, not long enough to make a connection. I had felt a connection to the Pacific, and it has always stayed with me. When I reflect on the Atlantic, I think about the ship and people. With the Pacific it is the opposite, it's all about the ocean, washing under me and over me and bringing me to the peace I was seeking in my life.

The intensity of the storms grew. What we had experienced thus far was tame in comparison. I was beginning to understand why such a giant ship could be delayed in reaching Wilmington.

The previous night, after my first visit outside, I had slept like a log. In fact, my best sleep since Mexico City. Tonight would prove to be a whole different story.

And it was not just stormy with heavy seas, it was also cold - real cold. As I looked out onto the bridge platform and down towards the deck, I could see ice forming. Waves over 20 metres were battering the ship as she ploughed forward to Europe. They seemed determined, those waves, to keep me from reaching home. One last twist, one last delay. But I was not deterred. Zorin and his boys were taking it all in their stride. They had seen the like before, and these few waves were not going to stop the greater enterprise that is commerce. The goods would be delivered and would be consumed at an ever-increasing rate.

As we passed close to Newfoundland, my telephone suddenly came to life. Ping, ping, and I had a signal. I took the opportunity to call my daughter and tell her I was safe and well and hoped to reach London in a week. Messages and emails started uploading until suddenly they stopped, the signal died and I was thrown back into communication blackout.

It felt good making contact to my former world for those brief minutes, knowing my family were safe and well. They were near and yet still so far. I was in Newfoundland, and they were in London. I was being thrown around on a cargo ship in storm-force weather. They were shopping in the King's Road, Chelsea, popping into Fratellis for a cappuccino. I grabbed yet another espresso and felt closer to them.

Day 59 Atlantic Tempest

In which the sea makes its full force felt to all on-board

"Life is full of misery, loneliness, and suffering - and it's all over much too soon." - Woody Allen

I knew there would be a time when I would think about life on the stormy Atlantic with something close to appreciation and longing, but today was not that day.

In total contrast to the previous night, I had hardly slept at all. At one point I was thrown off my bed. Over breakfast, Zorin asked if I had been seasick yet. He had a tiny smile on his face as he asked. I hated to disappoint him, but I had to say the truth. 'No, but it was a bit rough!' I loaded up a plate with eggs and toast and nearly off-loaded my breakfast on to him but managed to stagger back from the buffet table, falling down in my seat, rescuing my plate at the same time. It was indeed a bit rough!

Zorin had a mild look of surprise - I like to think of it as admiration or respect - as he told me half the crew had been ill from all the rolling around throughout the night. As I pointed out to him, 'Us British are made of sterner things, you know.' That definitely put a smile on his face. The fact was I had never been seasick in all my life, and I wasn't about to start now.

The forecast for the day was more of the same, and the consequence was that we would be arriving a day later than schedule. A day here, a day there. I was well within my *hoped for* 70 but slipping from the new target of 63 to 65 did hack me off a little. But what could I do? Travelling around the world was not a science, as Phileas had discovered. When he set off from London, he had no idea he would be travelling across India on an elephant, be pursued for theft, and find a princess bride. Travelling would throw up surprises from time to time. And that is a clear understatement.

Let's look at some of the facts on this journey alone, and let's get romantic for a while. Considering I was on the go and not dragging my feet, I had met Maja in Poland - she was a beauty, that's for sure. I had travelled through Siberia with Sofia - truly the creme-de-la-creme (what kind of fool am I)? In Mexico I had the encounter with the (in the future to be named) Turkish Tiger, Zeynep, followed soon after by my meeting the budding actress, Donna, on Venice Beach in L.A. And finally, I had run into the *wild girls* in Chicago. If someone had written that script for me before setting out, I would have laughed my head off. But it all happened, and those are just the romantic things. And without being too modest, I can say in all honesty that such situations occurred on almost every travel I have made.

So yes, travelling would throw up some odd surprises from time to time, and a seasoned traveller learns to accept them as part of the package. Being a couple of days late was not the end of the world. Being surrounded by border guards in Belarus was a bit left field, but no more so then ignorantly trying to join the Marines in North Carolina.

I could take a couple of days' delay in my schedule because of the raging Atlantic; I could take them in my stride. I was feeling quite good about life. The winning post was in plain sight, and I was galloping towards it. I was in a one-horse flat race (my dad would love that), and with no hurdles to jump, only the unseating of this jockey was going to prevent me from winning.

Day 60 Atlantic Ocean

In which today is the same as yesterday, and tomorrow is likely to be the same as yesterday also!

"But where, after all, would be the poetry of the sea were there no wild waves?" - Joshua Slocum

Storm after storm seem determined to throw me off course and delay my return to Europe, and the glory that awaits my slicing a couple of weeks off old Phileas' time.

As the days onboard pass and home beckons, my thoughts frequently drift to what awaits me. Endless hours on the bridge, staring into the raging seas, induce a kind of melancholy. I find I am less able to study or read; even exercising has lost its appeal - things that were so unforced and natural on the Pacific are becoming a chore on the Atlantic.

Perhaps the disquiet of the stormy waters is awakening storms within myself. I knew I had not yet made all the decisions I needed to regarding my personal life, and as I get closer to home, I know I cannot escape those issues which should be addressed.

How many people complain about not having enough time to think? Crossing these magnificent oceans provided thinking time many would envy, and yet I realise that thinking isn't a switch you turn on and off. Thinking needs thinking about - setting the right conditions. Being in the right frame of mind.

I have all the time in the world to think, and yet it's an act I have to consciously make myself do. The distraction of the weather and our slow progress through it doesn't help in the focusing department. I sit for hours on end, staring into the void, sometimes having to hold on for dear life as the ship crashes down into another wave, and the spray of biblical proportions travels over 200 metres to smash onto the bridge windows.

We have all heard of ships being lost at sea, and of extreme storms causing peril to sailors, but until you are in such a storm, it's impossible to fully comprehend. I'm tucked away on the bridge of a mammoth ship and think about how horrendous and frightening it must be for yachtsmen and fishermen, battling the elements to reach a safe harbour. They are surely either determined, stubborn or crazy - perhaps a little of all three. Did George Clooney know what he was getting into, sword-boat fishing on the Grand Banks and Flemish Cap in *The Perfect Storm*? We were passing close to those real-life locations, and I was more than thankful to be on a 200-metre plus ship and not the *Andrea Gail*.

I barely leave the bridge all day, only venturing away to eat lunch and dinner. Books and movies hold no interest for me. I stare mesmerised hour after hour, and occasionally my mind drifts back to some of the events of my journey thus far.

Day 61 Atlantic Social

In which the officers let their hair down on a *BIG* Saturday night on the *Independent Voyager*

"I know a man who gave up smoking, drinking, sex and rich food. He was healthy right up to the day he killed himself." - Johnny Carson

I'm not anti-social; I just don't like too many people too much. Let's say I'm selective. Life has taught me hard lessons about trust, and there are still lessons to be learned. My kids bought me a wall plaque that read *"There are two kinds of people in this world, and I don't like either of them"*. I love that plaque. I often wondered which one of those two people I was.

The days were winding down to arrival and return to *normal* life. Only four to go, and I would be taking the Eurostar back to the Old Smoke. London with all its life, energy, history and people; it really was one hell of a city, probably the best in the world. But it felt a million miles away from where I found myself now. Staring from the bridge of this massive cargo ship, looking out at the Atlantic Ocean, which was slowly, and thankfully, calming down again.

Glancing at the voyage route map, which showed the weather, I could see just what we had sailed through. And it wasn't pretty. Storm after storm were charted across most of the Atlantic. Thankfully, it looked like we were through the worst of it. *"Stormy Weather"* indeed, Etta James was on the money with those words. Sitting for hours staring at a vast nothingness, I could think of the storms I had recently navigated in life, and those that lay ahead. The past was done with, but a legacy always remains. The future storms would have to be dealt with, some quicker than others. I would be washing-down my decks pretty soon and seeking some calmer waters. The Pacific had shone its light on me. It had opened a door, and I fully intended to keep that door wedged open.

"It's seven o'clock and I wanna rock, Wanna get a belly full of beer." We met in the Officers' Recreation Room, and after a week of abstinence from alcohol, some of those Serbs were ready to let their hair down. They were ready to *rock*. I was ready to let mine down with them, and it proved to be a long evening, eventually winding up at around 2 a.m. It's fair to say quite a lot of booze was consumed. So, life on the *Independent Voyager* was, indeed, proving to be very different from the *Hanjin Athens*. Captain Schmidt would be blowing a fuse if he saw how this lot let rip.

I think that if anyone is going to be cooped up for so long on one of these ships, it's totally acceptable to let some steam off from time to time. No wonder some of the port calls get interesting. I was enjoying hanging out with these guys and would have loved to hit a couple of ports with them, if only to see just how wild they could be. Probably not like the *old days*, but fun was still out there to be had, if only you looked in the right place. And I was pretty confident Alex, Igor and Zorin would know where to look.

Day 62 Atlantic England

Where reaching home proves thought-provoking for Phil

"Be England what she will, with all her faults she is my country still." - Charles Churchill

Where is home? What makes us call a place home? Is it through birth, parents, family, friends or the place we stay the longest? Does home change? Can another place become home?

I spend my summers in Greece, and many Greeks who have lived for years in Australia and America come *home* every few years. Some come home to die. Why? Does a Greek really ever think of anywhere other than Greece as home? I have yet to meet one who does.

England is my home, and however long a time I may be away from her, she, with her green hills and rugged coastline, will remain so. And some of that coastline was not too far in the distance now. A day or so sailing and we would be entering the English Channel, en-route to Antwerp.

The closer I get to home, the more nervous I appear to be. And this is nothing to do with Phileas and beating his travel time or winning a bet. I knew when we left Wilmington, that my mission would be accomplished. No, it was to do with the end of this journey. The end of my time away from home. Perhaps we need to be away from places and people to fully appreciate them. Maybe my shipmates had successful relationships and appreciated their homelands more than most of us, simply because they were at distance from them for so long. I'm just surmising - maybe someone should study that?

I read a book about nostalgia once, someone who travelled away from home for some time. There are many books about nostalgia, but the one that struck me so much was *The Snow Geese* by William Fiennes. It's a simple book with a big impact. I've re-read it many times. I think I always will. It's not often a book leaves such an effect on me. Books, music, art, movies - what are we without culture? How empty would our lives be without culture filling the gaps of the everyday?

I was a little nostalgic for England, for home, my family and friends. But how much would I be missed if I just set off again from Antwerp and went around again? Would anyone notice, or anyone care? I was nostalgic, but perhaps more so for what I would be leaving behind, *On the Road*. It gets under the skin, travelling. And once it's there, the only thing you can do is scratch the itch from time to time. Since following in the footsteps of Phileas, I have scratched it a number of times, and as long as my ageing bones would permit, I'd keep scratching. Because, when you think you have seen everything, and think harder, you realise you've only scratched the surface.

Space. Now that would be a scratch. Probably one I would never make, but given the chance and the resources, I would be looking for a seat to the stars. Imagine seeing what those astronauts have seen. Sights that no camera could ever fully capture. Photographs show us so much, but also so little. We see them with one sense, but what of the other four? A couple of years later, I was travelling through Africa and reached Victoria Falls. My photos are reasonable, but what of the taste of spray on my tongue and feel of it on my face? And what of the deafening roar that my ears would never forget? And a few days later another roar, that of a lion as we got just a little too close.

I took many photographs of this journey around the world, but will they help tell my story? I shall leave it to others to decide whether they are included along with these words - assuming this story is published. And on that point let me say that my hand-written journal serves as the primary source of information to tell my story. Sure, my photos have helped, and I have undertaken a little research, but the real story, that is now unlocked from inside my head. It is that story I am trying to tell you. The story of what I remember, of what was left behind, when the journey was over.

Day 63 Atlantic Connected

In which every ping reminds Phil that he is so close to his old world

"There is nothing like returning to a place that remains unchanged to find the ways in which you yourself have altered." - Nelson Mandela

We entered the English Channel and headed towards Belgium. England, the place I call home so close and yet… no… home would wait for another day. And that day would come soon enough.

And as we crossed the busiest shipping lane in the world, we saw other ships. Some giants like us, many much smaller, and on reaching the far end, several ferries. Cornwall and Devon were within touching distance - the West Country. How many vacations had I spent there? Just a drive down the motorway, and *bingo*, an English summer holiday. I live in Devon now. Devon and Greece. Double *bingo*, life is a holiday. People tell me I'm lucky. Yes, I sure am.

The West Country is famous for its sailors and pirates. Famous for the Armada sent out by Elizabeth I to thwart the Spanish. Would I get nostalgic for all things connected to the sea? Is that why after a lifetime of talking about it, I would finally move to Devon, to be close to it? I even bought my first boat. Oh, it's very small, but it floats and moves, and often when I take her out, *Rough Justice*, past Dartmouth Castle, out into the open seas, I think of my time on the great oceans. I bob around, fishing for mackerel and far in the distance I may see a giant ship passing. Is she on her way to Antwerp, or heading west to America? Is she the *Independent Voyager?* They are too far away to discern, but they are there, passing every day. On average 500 vessels passing through those 350 miles, on their way to somewhere. To faraway lands. Every day.

I sometimes think it would be an idea to fly around the world. It would take just over 50 hours, but no… there's no sense in that. What would I see? Airports and clouds, and not much else. What would my senses experience? Cabin air, perhaps a snoring neighbour, plastic food and a very stiff body. No, flying would be no fun at all. I had spent many years - too many years - flying all over the world. Often on business trips, but cramped in the back, in a crumpled suit, eager to get off and into my first meeting. How did I do it? I really wonder. George Clooney did it in *Up in the Air*, and he seemed to love it, collecting his *air miles* along the way!

But the idea came to me as I looked out and up the Channel that I could fly but stop at as many places as possible that I had not yet visited. A *tick-them-off-the-list* trip. This was an idea that merited further thought.

We must have passed quite close to Blighty because suddenly my telephone pinged to life and 90 plus messages were uploaded. Back to reality. I don't recall that any of those messages were of any importance. Just the detritus of everyday life finding its way onto a machine, that seemed glued to my hand. A machine that was controlling our lives. How did we ever let that happen?

It would be my last full day onboard. A last supper tonight to press home my case to include George Best on the list of the five greatest footballers of all time. Zorin and Alex would fight their corner. I mean to say Johan Cruyff was good, but surely, he was not better than Georgie? I met him once, George Best, in a quiet little pub just off the King's Road, Chelsea. My *Blues* were playing his *Reds* on a sunny spring afternoon.

George wandered in and asked for a glass of orangeade. People looked in confusion, George had a reputation as a drinker. He was one of the friendliest people I ever met. Happy Irishman that he was - he strolled around the pub, shaking hands and saying hello to complete strangers. By half-time his beloved *Reds* were a goal down, and it could have been worse. I saw him order a pint and Whisky shot. Football can get to all of us, but to someone like George, I guess it was his way of life. Well, that and ripping up and partying, at any place he entered.

George was on my list whatever argument the Serbs put up. I bet none of them had ever met a real-life footballing legend. And he wasn't the only one for me, as I had also met one of the top three, Pele, and that was a day I will never forget either.

Day 64 Antwerp

In which arriving at your destination does not mean you have arrived at your destination

"I'm a big traveller these days. I was in Hong Kong. I live there. I was just in Belgium with my parents and now I'm on my way to North America. You will find me all over." - Jean-Claude Van Damme

We only reached our berth in Antwerp at 7 p.m. - we arrived 14 hours behind schedule. Partly due to the storms, but also there was a problem with a fuel switch overnight.

I had missed the last Eurostar train back to London, so decided it was best to stay on board, rather than drag my luggage around Belgium looking for a hotel.

My forced night on the *Independent Voyage* would be the last of my journey around the world. As we navigated the lock system that enables access to Antwerp port, I marvelled at the feat of engineering that could create such vessels and infrastructure. Long gone were the steamships and sailing schooners plying the world's oceans. Hundreds of those vessels' cargo loads could be transported on one of these new mammoths of the waves. As far as I could see, derricks and cranes filled the horizon and ships slowly positioned themselves to off-load their precious wares.

I was back to reality again, with a bump. No more bridge sitting days watching the endless seas, sometimes holding on for dear life as we crashed our way through another storm. No more soccer matches relived over dinner. No more exercise in a cramped and cold cabin. No more solitude.

Europe was bathed in spring sunshine for our arrival,

and it was a welcome relief from what we had endured in the crossing over. The Channel and Scheldt Estuary were calm and welcoming. In addition to navigating the locks it required three tugs to manoeuvre us through the port entrance. It was a long, slow process. I grinned and bore. London was calling, but she would have to wait one more day.

It wasn't long before the pings of my phone returned and announced my arrival back in the *real world*. But what is the real world? How much of this world do we really know or experience? I had crammed in a lot in 65 days, maybe more than most, fewer than some. I had gone all the way around and scratched the surface. Just a few scratches to show for my efforts, and a soon to be new tattoo on my arm, that opened a door to tell my tale to any inquisitive mind.

So, I enjoyed a second final supper with the officers and spent the evening on the bridge with those on duty, chatting. Most were staying on board for a return trip across the Atlantic. For them, a homecoming was still some weeks away. They had no complaints. It was the life they chose.

I would have hated it, stuck on that ship, that floating prison-home, yo-yoing across the Pond. But was it any harder a life than so many endured earning their buck? Probably not. It might take some getting used to, but once you had, well I guess it was better than commuting hours and working in a glass box of an office for years on end.

Exhausted, I descended to my cabin. A final night's sleep: and calm and peaceful it was. I was not in a massive rush the following day. *Big Ben* wasn't anxiously awaiting my arrival to proclaim me a winner. I settled in for the night, happy to have reached land, happy to be back in Europe, and nearly, oh so nearly, home.

Day 65 Home

In which Phileas Phil had completed his journey around the world in 65 days

"Why, I've just this instant found out that we might have gone around the world in only seventy-eight days." - Passepartout

And so, my journey reaches its end. My last day, and I didn't forget the one I gained, unlike Phileas; realising his error he dashed to win his bet. He also picked up a wife along the way - no such romance for me, unless we include Mexico, which was about lust, not love. Although I would argue I picked-up something much more valuable than romance from my travels.

I bade farewell to those football crazy Serbs. They had been a really good bunch, and my journey was a better one for having met them. Zorin, Alex and the rest of those *happy people*, those happy sailors. Whoever we have the good fortune to meet serve to enrich us, as we do them. Zorin promised to read Jules Verne's book one day, and I hoped that when he did, he would remember a modern-day Phileas arguing over who was the world's greatest footballer.

I clambered down the stairs. Would I ever board such a giant again? Would I feel the ocean's force driving me forward to realise my ambitions? It would be a few years later, steaming south to Antarctica across the Drake Passage, in another different kind of storm, that I was transported back with real meaning to that Atlantic crossing.

A taxi dropped me at the Brussels Eurostar terminal. Full circle back to the *Eurostar* train in Belgium. Those 65 days involving so many trains, and here I was again, taking the final journey back to London on one. I stood on the platform and images flashed back to me. Biala Podlaska in Poland, bumping into the beautiful Maja - Shenzhen, finding a helping hand in David, who guided me through immigration. A station whose name escapes me in Kansas, where I waited ten minutes, staring at the blue snow-capped mountains in the distance, and sucked in the cleanest of air, and marvelled at the nature all around me. And now Brussels station heading home, back to the big city and life as I had known it. The same life, but I was different.

As the train exited the Channel Tunnel, finally bringing me back to England, I realised I felt low. The fact was, that it was over. The high of achieving my objective had become a low at its ending. I had sated my wanderlust but would readily have continued along my merry way. My adventure had well and truly come to an end. I nearly cried. The Pacific had taught me how to cry again, how to let go and express myself in the most emotional of ways. However, I held in those tears and calmed myself, and let the English countryside pass; green and brown fields, one after another. Siberia had been white, only white snow laden expanses stretching as far as I could see. The colours of nature and the seasons in near and far off lands, ever-present, forever a wonder.

I thought of all those days alone, moving east, day after lonely day. Apart from a week on the Trans-Siberian with Sofia, I had been alone. And whilst it may have been a pleasant respite to have shared my time with someone, in general, I had to say I was pleased I had travelled alone. The impact of what I was doing, the places I saw and experiences lived through, were isolated to me. They were mine, and part of me wanted to keep them that way. They remain precious. I had religiously written a daily journal, and reading it this past winter, it has been a source of inspiration to write these pages.

It has taken me some years to write this account of my journey. Never sure of what stopped me, but something did; I held off bringing forward my memories, not knowing why. A few half-hearted attempts had been made, and quickly pushed aside. But now, in a relaxed and sunny Greece, I have taken a leap of faith and committed myself to the task of reliving, in as brutally an honest way as I can, those memories, those 65 unforgettable days. I don't expect anyone to use my journey as an example, or lesson of any kind. If I have any message to give, it is only to not allow our conventions of living life to limit our possibilities or horizons.

Phileas undertook his epic to win a bet. I had set out without fully understanding why I was trying to emulate him. But I now see that whatever my motive may have been, the end result was a lasting change that I have continued to try and evolve into a better me.

At midday, we pulled into St Pancras station, and this time I did hail a taxi to take me home. Some 65 days earlier, I had resisted the pull to return home and go on with my quiet life; resisted the idea to drop my plans for adventure. And I was so thankful that I had!

Slowly moving through the streets of London, I asked the taxi driver to go via the Reform Club in Pall Mall. One last homage to Monsieur Verne and Mr Fogg. We pulled up outside and the driver said, 'Are you a member?' 'No,' I answered, 'but I know someone who is.' We moved on and 15 minutes later, I was home. The concierge, Martin, greeted me by saying 'You've been gone a long time.' Indeed, he was right, I had been gone a long time.

Oh, how lucky I am to have such experiences, and believe me when I say that I never take that *lucky man* that I am for granted.

Phileas and Phil, world travellers, conquering epic journeys and revelling in excitement and adventures. Some 80 days reduced to 65, and it would have been shorter, had the Atlantic not played its stormy hand.

I have travelled far and wide over the years. From Antarctica to Africa, through Asia and South America and around Australia, but nothing has, or I expect will, match the sheer magnificence of those 65 days. From the traumas in Belarus to the American Wild West, and never to be forgotten double ocean crossings, I faced every emotion during those days and returned a changed man.

My journey, and especially the crossing of the Pacific, had given me peace of mind, and to this day that peace remains with me, a lasting testament to the power and wonder of travel.

If I may indulge a little with three quotes that sum up so much of what I feel following my journey around the world:

Wallace Stevens said, *"The most beautiful thing in the world is, of course, the world itself."* And I can tell you, he was spot on!

Confucius said, *"Wherever you go, go with all your heart."* My heart may well be much harder than I would like it to be, but it beats that little bit faster when I *go*.

And finally, Hans Christian Andersen, *"To move, to breathe, to fly, to float. To gain all while you give. To roam the roads of lands remote. To travel is to Live."*

Author's Note

"It's better to travel 10,000 miles than to read 10,000 books." - Chinese proverb

My journey around the world took 65 days, and with a little bit of good fortune, and a calmer Atlantic Ocean, could have been reduced to 63.

I travelled over the winter months of 2012/2013 and planned a four week break on reaching Hong Kong. I broke my journey from 20 December 2012 until 15 January 2013 - a total of 26 days. To be true to my objective, I checked the cargo vessel departures from Hong Kong to the U.S. and calculated back to London via the Trans-Siberian. Taking into account my planned stops in Berlin and Shanghai, I needed 15 days to reach Hong Kong. I therefore added 3 additional days in Hong Kong before boarding the *MV Hanjin Athens* to the States, hence that day is number 18.

If, like Phileas Fogg, I had simply gone for speed I could have saved one day in Berlin, three in Shanghai, and three in Hong Kong. I calculate the shortest possible number of days could have been 56. But what is the fun of travelling if you cannot see and explore? Yes, I was racing the clock, but I also had objectives to be achieved along the way. I was determined to cross a few destinations off my wish-list.

During the planned 26 day break I visited Kuala Lumpur, Sydney and Bali.

I left London on Wednesday 5 December 2012 and returned Wednesday 6 March 2013. A total of 91 days - less the 26-day break - I travelled for 65 days around the world.

www.blossomspringpublishing.com

Printed in Great Britain
by Amazon

76199953R00156